A Naturalist in Cannibal Land

A. S. Meek

(Editor: Frank Fox)

Alpha Editions

This edition published in 2019

ISBN : 9789353709938

Design and Setting By
Alpha Editions
email - alphaedis@gmail.com

This book is a reproduction of an important historical work. Alpha Editions uses the best technology to reproduce historical work in the same manner it was first published to preserve its original nature. Any marks or number seen are left intentionally to preserve its true form.

A NATURALIST IN CANNIBAL LAND

A CANNIBAL BELLE.

A NATURALIST IN CANNIBAL LAND

BY

A. S. MEEK

EDITED BY FRANK FOX

WITH AN INTRODUCTION BY
THE HON. WALTER ROTHSCHILD

AND THIRTY-SIX ILLUSTRATIONS

T. FISHER UNWIN
LONDON: ADELPHI TERRACE
LEIPSIC: INSELSTRASSE 20

First published in 1913

[*All Rights Reserved*]

PREFACE

MR. MEEK's connection with the Tring Museum dates back from the time when he tried his hands at ranching in Queensland. The collections he sent home from that country—and which I acquired from his father—pleased me so much that I gladly accepted his offer of making for my museum collections in the Papuan countries, being confident that A. S. Meek had the pluck and power of endurance necessary for a collector in those unexplored regions. My expectations have been amply fulfilled. The places visited have been numerous, the collections exceedingly rich in novelties and, last but not least, our intercourse with the traveller has always remained most pleasant.

When A. S. Meek left Queensland for New Guinea about the middle of the nineties, most of the places he proposed to visit were very little known. Since Wallace's famous exploration of the Malay Archipelago nearly all the travellers who went east with the special object of making zoological collections selected the Sunda Islands and Moluccas as their field of exploration, only a few of them going further east to the western and southern parts of New

Guinea. Although many of the day-flying insects and the birds—which are the objects most easily obtained by missionaries and officials with little experience in collecting, or by naturalists pressed for time—were already made known from the islands east of New Guinea and from the Solomons, the field was practically virgin to a great extent, particularly as regards moths. Even in the coast districts of the mainland of New Guinea no extensive moth-collecting had been done by any collector of experience. Considering the great zeal which A. S. Meek has shown throughout his travels, it cannot, therefore, be wondered at that the new species of moths discovered by him—many of which still await description —must be counted by the thousand.

Besides the Snow Mountains in Dutch New Guinea and a number of localities in British New Guinea at the north and south sides of the Owen Stanley Range, A. S. Meek has visited all the more important islands east and south-east of New Guinea as well as all the larger and many of the smaller islands of the Solomon group with the exception of Maleyta and Rennell, which he hopes to explore on another occasion.

The zoogeographical results of his expeditions to these little-known places are naturally of great interest. New Guinea, the largest island on the globe, lying under the Equator, and its mountain ranges rising to such heights that they are covered

PREFACE

with eternal snow, offers exceptional opportunities for the study of the vertical distribution of animals. The hot, steaming forests of the valleys and foothills and the sweltering bushland of the coast districts, are zoologically very different from the mountains, where the climate is cold and chilly mists envelope the landscape. At the medium and higher altitudes, from three or four thousand feet upwards, many of the lowland species are replaced by others which do not exist at lower elevations. One of the most surprising discoveries in these mountains is the large number of species of the butterfly-genus *Delias*, species with such brilliant colouring that one would associate them with a hot climate rather than with a cold Alpine district. These *Delias* are represented by different varieties and even distinct species in the various mountain ranges of New Guinea, testifying to the great age of the island. Only one or two of the species have near allies in Australia, while the islands around New Guinea have nothing which resembles the mountain species. The lowland species of Lepidoptera and other groups of animals, on the other hand, are generally of wider distribution.

This contrast between the species of the high and low altitudes of New Guinea will readily explain itself when the geological history of the island is better known. The explanation will probably be as follows:

New Guinea is evidently the remnant of a continent which has sunk beneath the sea for the greater part, only the higher elevations granting a refuge to the fauna and flora. When the land rose again to some extent, the newly-formed islands and the coast districts of the main island became populated by an invasion from the west, this new Malayan element in the fauna being, on New Guinea, most prominent in the lowlands and foothills, and extending far south in tropical Australia, whereas the original Papuan element is more evident at the higher altitudes than at the lower.

The largest and most beautiful butterflies of New Guinea are the metallic species of a genus best known as *Ornithoptera*, of which A. S. Meek had the good fortune of discovering several new ones, among them the largest of all butterflies, *Ornithoptera alexandrae*. I named this beautiful insect after her Majesty Queen Alexandra, it being a near relative of *Ornithoptera victoriae*. One of these metallic species, *O. priamus*, occurs from the Moluccas to the Solomons and New South Wales in orange, green, and blue varieties, another of them (*O. victoriae*) is found only in the Solomons, while no less than seven are restricted to New Guinea (*O. alexandrae, O. chimaera, O. goliath, O. meridionalis, O. paradisea, O. rothschildi,* and *O. tithonus*).

The rich, velvety-black garb of the male of these butterflies, ornamented with metallic green, blue and gold, reminds one strangely of the most conspicuous of the Papuan birds, the Birds of Paradise, famous for the brilliant or strange ornamental plumage of the males during the mating season. Only a few species of this bird family occur outside New Guinea (in Queensland and the Northern Moluccas), and it is very remarkable that none have been found on the Solomon Islands, the fauna of which is otherwise so closely related to that of New Guinea. As the Crown Pigeons (*Goura*), also characteristic of New Guinea, are represented in the Solomons by a miniature form, the *Microgoura* discovered by A. S. Meek, one might likewise expect some sort of Paradise bird to occur in the mountains of Guadalcanar or Bougainville. These mountains are as yet untouched by the collector. Meek postponed their exploration, partly on account of the difficulty of supply for a large camp far away from the coast, and partly because his time was taken up by the different islands of the Solomon group on which it was important to make collections. The Solomons, small as they appear on the map of an atlas, are a fascinating group for the naturalist. The majority of the species occurring are found on almost every one of the larger islands, but nearly every species has on each island some characteristic feature not met with in the specimens of that species obtained on any other island. This phenomenon of geographical variation is strikingly illustrated by the collections sent home from the Solomons by A. S. Meek. As we go from Bougainville in the north to Guadalcanar and San Christoval in the south, many species change in appearance, in some of the islands gradually, the stages in the modification being at times almost imperceptible, whereas on other islands the change is by leaps and bounds, the differences being generally most abrupt and greatest in the forms occurring on the New Georgia group of islets lying to the west of the main chain. If we now recollect that there are two opposing views on the evolution of species, the one view maintaining, with Darwin, that evolution took and takes place by a gradual modification of the species, and the other view asserting that new species spring up suddenly without intergradation with the parent species, the collections assume a profounder philosophic interest than if they were treated merely as an accumulation of rare, new or beautiful species.

Greatly as I have always been pleased with the results of Meek's expeditions, I have often regretted that his modesty prevented him from giving to the public some record of his experiences in countries which few or no white men had ever visited. We are therefore very glad that he has at last consented to do so.

Meek is a man who faces a danger bravely and then forgets all about it. He has been so long in Papua, exposed to the attacks of the natives, the vicissitudes of the climate, and the dangers of crossing the seas in a small schooner, that many times it was only by a hair's-breadth that he escaped from losing his life. He might have stirred the emotions of the reader by a dramatic description of such scenes as his shipwreck, when the wild breakers of the turbulent Pacific tossed and rolled him about helpless in the surf, now sucking him down head first, now throwing him over like a log, and literally smashing his boat to splinters,—or his flight from the camp of death in the mountains of Dutch New Guinea, when he lost several of his boys and was himself so ill that he wrote what he thought to be his last instructions, fully believing that he would not reach the coast alive. Such and similar experiences, however, Meek recounts in simple language without any attempt at adornment, and we think that the reader will like the traveller the better for it.

Before the book is in the hands of the public A. S. Meek will again be in the field, continuing his explorations in countries he has not yet visited, and in mountain ranges which are still virgin ground. At the Tring Museum we hope heartily that his intrepidity will carry our traveller safely through all the adventures which may await him on his new expeditions.

WALTER ROTHSCHILD.

Tring, February 1913.

EDITOR'S NOTE

WHAT I have been able to do to help this book to come to print has been a task of delight. Towards Meek, the naturalist, learned to distinguish varieties of butterflies by their down, I dare pretend to no great sympathy. My knowledge of natural history is slight. But for Meek, the explorer, who knows the wild places of the earth so well : who carries a charmed life among savages because he has neither fear nor cruelty; who talks simply of deeds of great daring—there is in my mind an almost envious admiration.

It is for its human interest chiefly that this story of a Naturalist in Cannibal Land seems to me of value; though, without a doubt, its scientific interest is very great, and on one scientific point all the world, ignorant and learned, will probably follow the author with attention : Is the tobacco indigenous to the hill country of New Guinea, or did a wave of colonisation from the American continent sweep across the Pacific, bringing with it tobacco before the dawn of history ?

The races among whom Meek has lived his adventurous life these 20 years are so rapidly passing away before the white man that every record of them in their primitive state is of intense interest. Engaging folk, mostly, these South Sea Islanders; at times gay, flower-bedecked, treating the stranger with the artless generosity of children; at other times sullen, passionate, wreaking the cruel, thoughtless revenges of vexed children; but always childish in temperament. They never needed to grow up. In the palm groves of their coral islands set in seas of sapphire, they lived before the European came as in Eden. Nature imposed no harsh conditions of labour. One lived to eat, to drink, and to be merry without vexations. The gorgeous butterflies flashing through the forests, the Birds of Paradise and Bower Birds dancing stately love-dances in their bowers, were typical of the human life of the islands. A little war, a little cannibalism, accentuated rather than broke the routine of indolent peace. Now the South Seas become like the rest of our world with the march of civilisation, carrying its blessings of work and wages, and disease and drabness of fettered life. It were wise to treasure this and every other truthful impression of the old order.

FRANK FOX.

London, 1913.

CONTENTS

CHAP.		PAGE
I	THE DESIRE FOR ADVENTURE	1
II	BEGINNING AS A COLLECTOR	27
III	MY FIRST EXPEDITION TO NEW GUINEA	42
IV	A TRIP TO THE TROBRIANDS	62
V	LEARNING TO NAVIGATE; AND SOME COLLECTING IN THE LOUISIADE GROUP	75
VI	A VISIT TO THE SOLOMON ISLANDS	96
VII	INLAND NEW GUINEA—THE NATIVES AND MEASLES	111
VIII	ANOTHER TRIP TO THE SOLOMONS—AND TO THE NEW GUINEA HILL COUNTRY	133
IX	SOME EXPERIENCES WITH THE NATIVES—TWO BOYS ARE MURDERED	152
X	COLLECTING ON THE GIRIWA RIVER	170
XI	THE SOLOMONS AGAIN: I GROW WEARY OF THE SOUTH SEAS LIFE	180
XII	AT THE FOOT OF THE SNOW MOUNTAINS	199
XIII	IN CENTRAL DUTCH NEW GUINEA	219
	INDEX	233

LIST OF ILLUSTRATIONS

	To face page
A CANNIBAL BELLE . . . . . . *Frontispiece*	
SAMARAI, PAPUAN MAINLAND IN DISTANCE	44
POLICE MAGISTRATE'S HOUSE, SAMARAI	45
A GAOLER, SAMARAI	46
BOAT BOYS, PAPUA	46
GOVERNMENT QUARTERS, SAMARAI	48
A HOUSE PARTLY EUROPEAN, PARTLY PAPUAN IN STYLE . .	53
SCENE, TROBRIAND ISLANDS	64
TROBRIANDER MAKING FISHING NETS	65
CHIEF'S HOUSE, TROBRIANDS	65
YAM HOUSES, TROBRIANDS	67
NATIVE GIRLS, TROBRIANDS	68
VILLAGE, TROBRIANDS	70
ALBINO CHILD, TROBRIANDS	71
PREPARING FOR A FEAST, TROBRIANDS	72
YAM STORES, TROBRIANDS	73
CEREMONIAL HOUSE, MILNE BAY	74
CANOE, TROBRIANDS	74
HOUSE, MILNE BAY	99
NATIVE CANOE, PORT MORESBY	109

xviii LIST OF ILLUSTRATIONS

	To face page
PORT MORESBY, PAPUA	110
PAPUANS WITH TOBACCO PIPE	115
NATIVE WOMEN WITH TOBACCO PIPES	116
THE KISS, PAPUA	119
A CHEERFUL LADY, PAPUA	123
WOMEN MAKING SAGO	155
JUNGLE, HILL COUNTRY, PAPUA	165
PAPUAN POLICE BOYS	167
DUBU, SOLOMON ISLANDS	185
PRISON AND PRISONERS, SAMARAI	195
PRISONERS AT WORK, SAMARAI	196
DUTCH EXPLORERS' CAMP, OETAKWA RIVER	211
CANOE CAMP, OETAKWA RIVER	213
DUTCH OFFICERS' QUARTERS, ISLAND RIVER	219
DUTCH EXPLORERS' CAMP, ISLAND RIVER	219
MY CAMP UNDER THE SNOW MOUNTAINS, DUTCH NEW GUINEA	223

A NATURALIST IN CANNIBAL LAND

CHAPTER I

THE DESIRE FOR ADVENTURE

SOMETIMES when I look through the catalogues of the great Tring Museum and see so many butterflies and birds with " meeki " as specific names, I confess I feel a little ashamed, as though I were sailing under false colours. These insects and birds named after me seem to proclaim that I am a scientist; and that, I cannot honestly claim to be. The honour of those names I have not really earned. The desire for an adventurous life rather than a passion for science has been the guiding principle of my life. When I am asked how I came to be a naturalist I am inclined therefore to disavow the title, and to answer that I am more a lover of wild life and a student of nature than a scientific observer.

My father, it is true, was a naturalist; professionally so, for he made his livelihood for many years as a dealer in Natural History specimens, and as a collector of British lepidoptera. I have early recollections of going out collecting with him on various expeditions in different parts of the British

Islands, but I do not think that I can honestly say that as a boy I took any particular interest in the collecting. It was rather the open-air life that appealed to me. Still I must have inherited some scientific curiosity, and my father did his best to encourage this with such rewards as appeal to the young. I have an early recollection of getting up before the summer dawn to collect in Hyde Park the little yellow insect known as the "thorn." My father had offered me sixpence for every black specimen of this common moth that I brought to him. I never earned a sixpence, though on two occasions I saw a black specimen, but on neither occasion made a capture. Another early ambition of mine was to get a black specimen of the black-and-white moth known as the "gooseberry" moth. I used to collect the larvæ of this moth in Hyde Park and then hatch them out. For a long while all the moths came out true to type, until finally one hatched out a steel-grey colour, and this specimen was worth three guineas. It was of course a freak. I have often bred two or three thousand larvæ of a particular insect before getting a freak specimen.

My most pleasant memories of boyhood are associated with trips to the New Forest collecting butterflies and moths, generally by means of sugaring the trees. We would cover a number of trees with a mixture of treacle and beer and essence of pear, and then go round with a lamp at night to collect the specimens which had been trapped in this sticky mixture. When I recall those early collecting trips of boyhood I think of the strange difference between that method of collecting—never far from a railway station, living in a village inn—and my present life, which makes it necessary to plunge into a trackless forest and cut oneself off from civilisation for many months at a time. In the New Forest we never slept in a tent, never, to my recollection, cooked a meal in the open air. There was nothing of the "wild life" in such collecting. But I suppose that if I had had any real scientific enthusiasm it would have appealed to my interest. It did not. It was more pleasant than living in London; but I dreamed always of the savage lands of my boyhood's books.

The Natural History of the British Islands, so far as lepidoptera is concerned, was fairly familiar to me by the time I had reached the age of fourteen, but my father did not allow collecting trips to interfere with school life. During the holidays he would take me to different parts of the country on these collecting trips, but during school terms I was obliged to stick closely to the desk, without much love for letters except insomuch as they helped me to read stories of adventure. My father on occasions took collecting trips on behalf of private collectors to Madeira and the Canary Islands, but I was never allowed to accompany him abroad.

At fourteen I left school, intending (or rather,

obedient to my father's intention) to enter a college; but that intention was never carried out. I managed very artfully to let the holidays drift on month after month, making myself useful to my father in his workroom, always "going to school again next term," but never going. Then finally, after a great deal of persuasion, I was able to induce my father to give up the idea of college life for me, and he allowed me to help him more in his collecting trips, and to be of some assistance in setting insects for his collections. I do not know whether it was with any conscious desire on my part at this time to fit myself for life in savage lands, but I can recall my particular devotion to a gymnasium near by, which I haunted every night, and kept myself thus very fit. To that early love for the gymnasium and the habit I acquired there of taking regular exercise, I owe probably my degree of immunity from tropical diseases. Nowadays I get fever very often in the New Guinea swamps. But it does not prostrate me to the same extent as most. When I leave the malaria country I do not take the fever away with me, and to-day I feel vigorous and healthy after some twenty years of the hardest possible life in the jungles and the mountains of tropical Oceania.

Natural History was not at this time altogether neglected. I was often at the Natural History Museum, Kensington. My father would send me there with specimens of insects to have them named.

I can remember often seeing the Hon. Walter Rothschild there. His passion for entomology was even then keen, and he was often in my father's place looking over collections. I did not dream then that I would one day be stationed at the Antipodes to collect for him, but always I kept the hope in my heart of getting away somehow from the narrow life of the city.

When I reached the age of seventeen there came the first promise of this. My father arranged to take me to the Canary Islands on a collecting trip. We were preparing for this trip when a letter came from Mr. George Barnard, of Coomooboolaroo Station, Queensland. He was a squatter, or rather cattle-rancher, who followed up a scientific enthusiasm for entomology in that far-away corner of the earth; my father was in the habit of supplying him with butterfly cabinets, and had once written to him asking him if there were a chance in Australia for a young man with a desire for an open-air life and some knowledge of Natural History. Mr. Barnard had now written in reply that he thought he had sufficient influence to get me into a museum in Australia. Truth to tell I was not particularly joyful at the prospect of working in a museum, but the idea of Australia was attractive. It was a concession to the roving spirit in my blood. That letter came in March of 1889. By April I had left for Australia by a British India Company's boat.

We landed at Rockhampton, Queensland, after seven weeks' voyage, during which I got my first sight of savage people. Thursday Island, which gave me this first knowledge of tropical life, was at that time a particularly interesting place. Now its glory has mostly departed, but it was then the great centre of the pearling fleet in Australian waters. That was in the days before the Japanese had come into the pearling industry, and all the chief divers were white men who had under them as helpers South Sea Islanders. The white divers usually led reckless and extravagant lives. The custom was to spend three weeks at work and then to waste six weeks in a wild spree on shore. Thursday Island was the usual centre for these revels, and I suppose that was how it got its name corrupted in the popular tongue to "Thirsty Island." The pearl shell beds then were very rich, and lay in shallow waters, so that the yields were very good. When pearl shell could be got at a depth of twelve or fifteen fathoms, a diver could stop down collecting it all day. Now, when the fishing is in deeper water, it is impossible to get anything like such good yields, and most of the pearling fleet have left Thursday Island for new headquarters in the Dutch Indies.

From Rockhampton I went by train to Duaringa, and then fifteen miles further on to Coomooboolaroo Station. At that station I stayed as the guest of Mr. Barnard for some four months, and I think those branding, mostly young calves, who of course had to be got out with their mothers. The usual mode of doing this was to pick on a site for a small camp away from the main cattle camp, and having got out a beast with its calf, to leave her there and gradually get the nucleus of a little herd consisting entirely of mothers with their calves. Having got together a good mob of young cattle for branding, the next task would be to drive them to the cattle yards near the homestead, and the cattle we had collected in the big cattle camp would be allowed to disperse among the ranges again.

Work among cattle requires smart, plucky riding. One advantage to the cattle man is that his horses know a great deal about the game. But this is not an advantage always to the new chum. I have often noticed an English rider, perfect for taking a horse over all sorts of country in England, finding himself quite at sea in cattle country, for the reason that he does not understand that the horse knows the ways of the cattle, and will follow its own bent rather than be guided blindly by his rider. All the big accidents that I have known in riding after cattle have been caused by a difference of opinion between the horse and his rider as to which was the better side of a tree to pass on. When a difference of opinion of this sort crops up and both horse and rider are stubborn, the usual result is to land them head on to the tree, possibly with cracked skulls or broken necks. But the average accident with cattle is not so serious as that. It is more humorous than serious, and is due to the fact that the rider is not prepared for some sudden wheel on the part of the horse, and comes off, ungracefully but without suffering much damage. Horses that are used for cattle work get to love the game quite as much as their riders, and also get to understand its points quite as well. At Coomooboolaroo our daily rule was to muster one day, to brand the cattle the next day, and on Sundays to take holidays of a sort. Usually we put in Sunday bathing in the lagoon, and collecting Natural History specimens.

But in those days the collecting was not for me a very serious matter. Australian territory had been covered so thoroughly that there was not much new material to discover, and I cannot recollect making a single Natural History find of any value during my stay at Coomooboolaroo. But that stay was extremely valuable to me in teaching me the ways of horses and the bush lore in which the Australian cattle man is so much of an adept. When I came later to undertake expeditions into the wildest parts of New Guinea, I had reason to be grateful for the grounding in the ways of the Bush which I had got in Australia.

Life at Coomooboolaroo was indeed very pleasant. Mr. Barnard was the best of good fellows, and his place was a particularly comfortable example of a cattle station. There was a fine garden attached to

THE DESIRE FOR ADVENTURE 11

the homestead, and we had plenty of fruit and vegetables and milk and butter and cream to eke out the salt beef. That was the usual meat ration, except when a beast was killed, about every fortnight, when fresh beef was available. On the Queensland cattle stations it is the custom also to get a small herd of goats for meat. A fat goat, if it is not too old, makes excellent eating. To my mind goat mutton is quite as good as sheep mutton.

I had not been a week on Coomooboolaroo Station before it had become quite clear to me that I did not want to go into any museum. The thought of sitting in an office, of living in a city, of working at a desk, was to me now quite intolerable. But my host at Coomooboolaroo, who treated me with a degree of kindness of which I shall always cherish grateful memories, thought that it was not a fair thing for me, as a youngster with his way to make in the world, to waste my time on his station. He liked, as he said, to have me there, but there was no future good or present profit to be got out of life there for me. Finally he got me a position on a sheep station outside Hughenden, telling me that if I was determined to stick to the country life it would be well for me to see something of the work on a sheep station. At Hughenden of course I was an employee, and got some wages, and I suspect that Mr. Barnard's idea was that I should find life there so different that I would be glad to give up the Bush and turn to following my father's plans and seek a post in a museum. But in that idea he was wrong.

The sheep country in Australia is very different from the cattle country. Generally speaking, the more remote parts, or the rougher forest parts, are devoted to cattle, while the plain country and the country near the railways is given up to sheep. At Redcliff Station, where I had now become a "jackeroo," that is to say, a youngster learning the business of wool growing, the country was partly plain with Mitchell grass and partly gidyea scrub. The plain was covered with deep black soil, and after the rains would produce grass most luxuriantly. In the dry season it would be quite bare, and would crack up in all directions like the bottom of a dried-up clay pit. If you saw the Black Soil Plains of Australia in a time of dry weather you would not think it possible that any green thing could grow there, but after the first shower of rain herbage comes as if by magic. The grass follows, and if the rain has been heavy the vegetation will grow up very quickly to the height of a man.

The evils of the great droughts which afflicted Australia in the old days were caused by pastoralists estimating the value of the country for carrying sheep during the times when the grass was most plentiful. When the grass dried off there were too many sheep for the land to supply with food, and the result was very serious loss. Nowadays over-

THE DESIRE FOR ADVENTURE 13

stocking, as it was called, is not so common, and on many stations the very luxuriant vegetation of the summer is stored up in pits called silos as a safeguard against dry times. I do not think that in these times there could ever be very serious loss from drought in Australia, at any rate not such loss as used to be met with in the old days, when on one station that I knew a quarter of a million of sheep perished of thirst and starvation.

Work at Redcliff was not by any manner of means easy. My duties as a "jackeroo" were various. I had to help to muster sheep, to repair fences, to do odd jobs of blacksmithing and to be a general utility man. The number of things which the Bush worker of Australia must turn his hand to is something wonderful. It is not at all unusual to find a Bush worker who is a fairly good carpenter, something of a wheelwright and a blacksmith, with a thorough knowledge of horses and cattle. And all these virtues are rewarded by a wage which is not very much higher than that of an English artisan.

At Redcliff I had an opportunity of studying the cunning to which a horse can attain. We were much overworked. Often my mate and I would be roused long before daylight to get in the horses in order to start work. I would have to go out into the night paddock to find the night horse in the dark. He had as much objection to such early rising as I had, and since I could not see him he would, by keeping very still and not allowing his bell to ring, dodge me until it was dawn. Sometimes at this station I was for long spells fifteen or sixteen hours in the saddle every day. I got thus absolutely sick of the sight of horses. The work on a sheep station, too, was dull and unexciting after my experience with the cattle. The cattle life appealed much more to the imagination than life among the sheep, which is mostly hard, dull work.

I can sympathise with that jolly versifier of the Australian bush, poor Harry Morant, in his disgust over the cattle run which had been turned into a sheep station:—

" Young Merino bought the station, fenced the run and built a shed,
Sacked the stockmen, sold the cattle, and put on sheep instead;
But he wasn't built for Queensland, and every bloomin' year
One hears of labour troubles when Merino starts to shear.

There are ructions with the rouseabouts, and shearers strike galore :
The like was never heard of in the cattle days of yore;
Whilst slowly round small paddocks now the sleepy lizards creep—
And Goorybibil's beggared since the country carried sheep !

They've built bush yards on Wild Horse Creek, where in the morning's hush
We've sat silent in the saddle, and listened for the rush
Of the cleanskins—when we heard 'em it was ' wheel 'em if you can,'
While gidgee, pine, and mulga tried the nerve of horse and man !

.   .   .   .

From sunrise unto sunset through the summer days we'd ride—
And stockyard rails were up and pegged with cattle safe inside,

THE DESIRE FOR ADVENTURE 15

When 'twixt the gloaming and the dark we'd hear the welcome note
Of boist'rous, pealing laughter from the kookaburra's throat.

Camped out beneath the starlit skies—the treetops overhead,
A saddle for a pillow and a blanket for a bed,
'Twas pleasant, mate, to listen to the soughing of the breeze
And learn the lilting lullabies that stirred the mulga trees.

Our sleep was sound in those days, for the mustering days were hard—
The morrows might be harder, with the brandings in the yard!
But did you see the station now—the men! and mokes! they keep—
You'd own the place was beggared—since the country carried sheep!"

The "boss"—to use the Australian word—of this sheep station was a believer in getting all he could out of a horse as well as out of a man, and I earned my dismissal there because he thought that I was not quick enough in going about a particular job that he had given me. I recollect riding there my first outlaw horse, an animal named "Grasshopper." (It curiously enough was responsible for the death of my boss some months after I left the station.) The experience of "buck-jumping" was not particularly disconcerting to me. At any rate I was not thrown out of the saddle, though until I had arrived in Australia I had never had my leg across a horse.

After leaving Redcliff, compulsorily, I took a job on a cattle station as a stockman. At this station the owner was anxious to breed horses for India, and he had some very good stock on his place, of which he was extremely careful. I am afraid that I had picked up from my last boss some rough ideas of my duties to a horse. At any rate I did not satisfy the manager of this cattle station, being accused by him of riding a horse too hard and spoiling it. Yet in those days in Australia (it was before the Indian trade had been well worked up), a good horse could be got for £2 or £3.

I had now reached the age of eighteen. I had had four months of the most jolly life possible as a guest at Coomooboolaroo Station and then a few weeks of experience as a Bush worker, during which time I had earned dismissal, or what the Australians call the " sack," twice. At least if I had not earned it I had got it, and now at the age of eighteen I was called upon to face the future without any very definite prospects ahead of me. It was of course possible for me to go back to my friends at Coomooboolaroo, but that was open to the objection that I would appear rather as a failure. So I dismissed that idea from my mind. It was also possible for me to seek a post in connection with a museum where my entomological knowledge would have been valuable, but that idea was not entertained for a moment. I was in love with the wild life of the " back country " of Australia. I had a few pounds in my pocket and I cheerfully went out on the tramp to look for work.

In Australia this tramping in search of work is

THE DESIRE FOR ADVENTURE

known as " humping bluey," and seeing that it was in the middle of my first Australian summer, in the hottest part of the Continent, I think that my love of the wild life must have been very strong to enable me to put up with the hardships which I encountered. I was not skilled in the ways of the country, or I should never have attempted to " hump bluey " walking. Since horses were so cheap I might easily have bought one, and travelled about in search of work much more comfortably. Ignorance, however, sent me on my travels on foot. Now of course, with my knowledge of Australian life, I would never dream of tramping the " back country " on foot if I had any possible means of getting a horse. Among the seekers for work in the " back country " the aristocrats are the horsemen, and to go in search of work afoot shows usually that you have come down very much in the world. Well, I " humped bluey " for some six weeks, walking in all quite three hundred miles of the plain country in the interior of Queensland. During the whole of the time I never thought once of going back to London or of seeking work in a city. One day, about Christmas-time, with the thermometer, I am sure, registering at least 100° in the shade, I walked quite thirty-five miles with my swag. I added to my knowledge of life on this tramp by learning to swim. The wet season had come and the rivers were all up. For three days I was kept waiting once for a river to go down, and I took the opportunity to learn to swim in a back-water, or billabong, as the Australian word is.

Many of the men in the "back country" of Australia who tramp from one station to another do not wish for steady work. They are known as "sundowners" because they try to shape their movements so as to arrive at a station at sundown. It is the custom for most stations to give a "sundowner" rations sufficient to support life for a day. Thus it is possible to tramp the "back country" without having either work or any means. But during my six weeks of "humping bluey" I never cadged for tucker. Having £6 or £7 in my pocket I was able to buy what I wanted.

Finally, at a station called Elderslie on the Diamintina River, I got a job repairing some fences which had been knocked down by the floods. While there I saved a little money, and having received some more money from my father in England for the Natural History specimens that I had sent home, I made up my mind to strike out on my own. I bought a horse and a gun and joined a kangaroo-shooting party in the Bladensburg ranges outside Winton. Kangaroo-shooting was at that time a fairly profitable occupation. The kangaroos were so numerous as to be a pest to the pastoralists, and so it was the custom to pay a bonus of 2s. for each kangaroo destroyed. On producing the scalp of a kangaroo at the Land Board Offices you were able to draw

THE DESIRE FOR ADVENTURE

the bonus, and you had still the hide of the animal for yourself, and that was worth 12*s*. or 13*s*. for leather.

It was probably rather a bold thing for me to undertake kangaroo-shooting without having had any particular practice, either as a bush-man or as a shot. But I was one of a party which included several experts, and seeing that each of us got his returns in accordance with the number of kangaroos he had shot, there was no injustice to my mates in my incompetence. It simply meant that I shot fewer kangaroos and earned less money.

In this, my first independent enterprise, I did not make a fortune, but the life was very jolly, and I was able to do a little Natural History collecting at the same time as I was shooting kangaroos for their pelts. Kangaroo-shooting would hardly be classed as a sport, however. There was not much idea of giving a sporting chance to the kangaroo. Our system was to make moccasins of bullock-hide with which to cover our boots so as not to make a noise. We would then slink round the gidyea scrub on the look-out for kangaroos and shoot them as they squatted. The kangaroos would keep to the gidyea scrub during the hot hours of the day, making wallows for themselves in the dust, and come out in the evening and early morning to feed. By following up the edges of the gidyea scrub we were able often to intercept the kangaroos on their way from the feeding-grounds to their haunts in the scrub. Sometimes we encountered the kangaroos lying in their wallows. Then the unfortunate kangaroo would be shot as it sat. If the kangaroos were encountered on the move, the plan was to attract their attention so that they would stop out of curiosity for a moment. That moment would be taken advantage of by the shooter.

It was not sport; it was shooting for gain. Some of the men would get five or six kangaroos in a day. The kangaroos seemed to be very stupid. If you shot one of a mob in a wallow, you could be sure, by going the next day, to find the remainder of the mob back in the same place. They never seemed to learn that a spot was dangerous. When the kangaroos were shot they would be skinned at once, and we would bring the skins back to camp and peg them out there. Sometimes if meat were short in the camp one of us would bring back the tail of a kangaroo, the only part of the animal which is usually eaten. The usual weapon used was a 44° Winchester. Altogether I stayed in the kangaroo-shooting camp some three or four months, during which time I sent out to my father many specimens for stuffing of kangaroo, wallaby and wallaroo skins.

It was probably the undertaking of this amount of collecting that revived in me some enthusiasm for Natural History. At any rate I took the opportunity of an invitation that was given to me to go back to

THE DESIRE FOR ADVENTURE 21

the cattle station at Coomooboolaroo, where I stayed for some twelve months acting as a stockman on wages in the main, but doing a great deal of collecting of insects and birds in the brigalow scrub surrounding the station.

Then, partly with the idea of collecting in a different type of country, partly moved by the roving spirit, I took a job as stockman at the Peak Vale Station, Peak Downs, in the far west of Queensland. I was on an out-station called Keilambete, where Mr. Walter Barnard, the son of my friend, was manager. He, I, a Kanaka stockman and a Chinese cook, were the staff at this out-station. The type of cattle work there was much wilder than at Coomooboolaroo. We would take pack-horses out for a three- or four-days' trip, mustering in the scrub. There was only one cattle yard used on the station, and most of the cattle we went out after were "scrubbers," that is to say, wild cattle used to life in the scrub. Our system was to have near to the station a few quiet cattle who acted as coaches or decoys to the wild cattle. We would drive these quiet cattle to some place suitable for a cattle camp, leave them there and then scour the country for a mob of wild ones. When the wild ones were mixed up with the tame cattle we would drive the whole lot to the one cattle yard which the station possessed, and there brand all the " clean-skins," and also unsex all the beasts, male and female. The cattle would then be turned out into the scrub again until they were wanted for the fat stock market.

The mustering of scrub cattle for branding is exciting work. It is a game that horses simply love. You may notice them when you are out in the scrub after cattle, watching with eager eyes and straining necks for a sight of the cattle. When they have sighted them there is no need for whip or spur. The horse is on the hunt like a flash, and if you are not used to the ways of cattle you are out of the saddle like a flash.

When out after scrubbers the idea is to cut the cattle off from any thick scrub. Once they are in a thick scrub it is almost impossible to get them out. But in the open you can always manage them. It is, however, delicate work getting them on the move. The idea that some artists who picture cattle-droving seem to have—viz., that the drovers urge the beasts on with galloping horse and flogging whip is of course absurd. You coax a mob on very gently, relying upon the quiet cattle to keep the wild ones in something like order.

At this station, Keilambete, I had a first experience of "moonlighting" cattle. The wild scrub cattle were accustomed to come down at night to the waterholes to drink. On moonlight nights we would bring up a small mob of quiet cattle to the waterholes, and try to manage things so that the wild ones coming down to the water would get mixed up with

THE DESIRE FOR ADVENTURE

the tame ones, and then the whole mob would be got into the cattle yard and the " clean-skins " branded.

I never had an opportunity of doing any very long droving trips, though I have often taken cattle down from Coomooboolaroo to the market—quite a short trip. The really fine droving experience is the " overlanding " trip from the cattle stations on the Gulf of Carpentaria to the New South Wales Fat Stock Market. It is called " overlanding," I suppose, because there is an alternative method of sending the cattle from these Gulf stations by steamer to New South Wales. An " overlanding " drove will sometimes occupy about three months. It is usual to travel the cattle about seven miles a day. They, of course, graze as they travel. There are what are called stock-routes along which the cattle must travel, and they are permitted to wander half a mile on either side of the stock-route. It is a grand sight to see a full mob of cattle, say 1000 or 1100 on the road, especially when they have broken into a gallop. Droving, of course, is quite an organised industry in Australia and can be made very comfortable. Usually the head drover has a plant consisting of a dray and tents and a staff of seven or eight men. Under these circumstances the night camps can be made comfortable and, as it is only necessary for one or two men to keep a guard at night, everybody can have a decent allowance of sleep.

A thunderstorm at night is the chief terror of the

Overlander. The man in charge has seen the mob quietly settled down, and with two of the stockmen has turned in for sleep. One is left to take the first watch; his duty will be to see that the horses of the others are ready for quick saddling and an instant start, and to ride round and round the camping cattle until at midnight he can wake up the relief sentry.

As night deepens the man on watch is conscious of a strange sultriness. The cattle notice it too, and the mob stirs uneasily. Here and there comes a faint low. The Overlander is at once all alert. He takes a glance at the tethered horses to see that they are all right; then he rides round the herd, singing or whistling as he does. The human voice seems to bring some quiet to the uneasy beasts whose animal sense has told them that a storm approaches.

A green-black cloud shows on the horizon, blotting out the stars as it creeps higher and higher into the sky. Low rumblings sound and the faint flashes of distant lightning show behind the cloud. There is a swelling of wind. Many of the cattle are now on their feet, sniffing towards the coming storm, stamping on the ground with their hoofs. From one beast comes a bellow of fright.

The Overlander knows now that he must act. His mates are aroused; within three minutes they are in the saddle, circling around the mob. One sings "The Wild Colonial Boy," another "Wrap me up

THE DESIRE FOR ADVENTURE 25

in my old Blanket"; from another perhaps you hear "What care I how fair she be, if she be not fair to me?"

The cattle seem easier. The Overlanders begin to think again of sleep.

Suddenly a blinding flash, a smash of thunder, a great roar as of pain, fury and fear from the cattle, and they are away in a wild stampede. On the far skyline is a forest of belar trees; for this they are making. Reaching it, they will, many of them, be killed and lost. That must, at all costs, be prevented.

The men know, the horses know what is to be done. In the black darkness, rent now and again by lightning, through the stinging rain, the Overlanders rush at a stretching gallop to "head the mob." On either wing two horsemen fly, and as the moments pass get in front of the cattle. Then a quick wheel right and left, and with whips lashing, voices cursing, they are heading the maddened beasts. It is for a while a running fight. The horsemen must not get too near to the cattle as to be trampled underfoot. They must get so near that their voices and their whips may be felt. Finally the men win. The cattle hesitate, turn back. Now they are safe. They will be kept moving whilst the storm lasts, but it will be a quiet and an ordered movement.

The life has enough of adventure to satisfy any man; enough of shared danger to bring out the best in any man. I would have been willing enough to have stayed on as a cattle man but that I had no hope of becoming my own boss in that capacity.

At Keilambete Station I had saved some money, and when quite a big amount came from home for the collections I had sent forward, I made up my mind to start a regular life as a naturalist collector. Life on the cattle station was very good fun, but it did not promise any very good fortune. I was now twenty-one, and beginning to look to the future. It was necessary to make an end of " cattle collecting."

CHAPTER II

BEGINNING AS A COLLECTOR

I HAVE never regretted that first year I spent in Australia on cattle and sheep stations, tramping the bush, kangaroo-shooting. It was a jolly, irresponsible time, full of adventure and excitement; and it hardened me off finely for the sterner work that was ahead.

Mr. W. B. Barnard, a son of my friend, joined forces with me for the first expedition which I made purely for purposes of collecting. We went to Rockhampton, bought an outfit and then took a camp up in the ranges near Coomooboolaroo, staying there for three months. For the first time I had a regular collecting outfit, insect boxes, and arsenic for skins. Nowadays I do not trouble to use arsenic for preserving skins, but rely on alum, and on the use of plenty of naphthaline in packing up the skins. On this expedition we were out after all kinds of specimens—mammals, birds, and insects. I had secured through my father an order from the Hon. Walter Rothschild for three pairs of every kind of animal, whether mammal, bird, or insect that we collected. I had been collecting in a desultory kind of way all the time I had been in Australia, but on this trip I made for the first time collecting the only object of life. Unfortunately my mate suffered a good deal from rheumatism, and had to abandon the camp once for quite a long spell, leaving me alone there. That was an experience which at first I found a little unpleasant. But it fell to me so often afterwards that I think nothing now of being the only white man in a camp among savages six weeks' march away from the next white neighbour.

On this, my first collecting trip, I made not many new discoveries. I do not think it was possible to have done so, as from a Natural History point of view that part of Australia had been very well explored, at least as regards birds and butterflies. We collected, however, some interesting specimens, especially of the flying squirrels. Then, in search of something new, we went up the Johnson River, Queensland, making a camp about ten miles from the mouth of the river. Again we collected everything in the way of Natural History specimens—mammals, birds, and insects. I think I must except crocodiles, which were very plentiful there, but which we did not trouble to collect. I recollect once, when out shooting ducks in a swamp which kept us up to our waists in water, I came upon a crocodile's nest with fifty-seven eggs in it. This nest was made of swamp grass and the eggs in it were all together higgledy-piggledy. The eggs of the crocodile are hatched out by the heat

BEGINNING AS A COLLECTOR

from the fermentation of the vegetable heap in which they are laid. The Australian scrub hen also lays her eggs in a vegetable heap, relying on fermentation to bring the young out, but in the case of the scrub hen all the eggs are separated from one another by layers of vegetation. There are several variations in the method of depositing eggs among those creatures which trust to natural agencies and not to brooding for the hatching out. The crocodile, as I have said, makes a vegetable mound and lays the eggs in a heap, and covers them over with more vegetable matter. The female turtle lays her eggs in a heap in the sand. The black iguana (the carrion iguana) deposits her eggs in a white-ants' mound, and leaves them there to be hatched out. The sand iguana, which does not live on carrion, lays its eggs in the sand. The crocodile, by the way, is very fond of the eggs of the scrub hen, and will often travel far inland searching for the nests.

I never thought of danger in connection with the crocodiles in Northern Australia, but there is no doubt that they occasionally get a human victim. In the warm weather the crocodiles sleep in the scrub a little away from the water during the day. In the winter they sleep on the mud flats of the swamps. They usually feed in the evening, and that is the dangerous time for those who go near their haunts.

Perhaps some notes on the habits of the mound-building birds encountered in Australia and the

South Sea Islands will be of popular interest, though of course scientifically they are not new. The two families of mound-building birds in Australia are the scrub turkey and the scrub hen. Several varieties of each are found in Australia and in some of the South Sea Islands. The scrub hen makes a very large nest, returning year after year to the same mound and building it to a great size. In the Solomon Islands these birds have been almost domesticated, and their mounds are counted in the property of a tribe. The fermentation of the mound hatches out the eggs, and when the chicken breaks the shell it lies on its back and scratches its way out of the mound. It may be of interest to observe that there is no difference in the plumage of the male and female in the scrub hen.

One may encounter the scrub hen right through Polynesia. The scrub turkey is only found in Australia and New Guinea. I have met with two kinds of scrub turkey in Australia. One, which is only found in the north at Cape York, breeds on the tops of mountains, making a very shallow nest. In the case of this bird the head is red and the wattles on the neck are white. The other variety of scrub turkey I have met with in Central Queensland. It makes its nest in the brigalow scrub. The head is red but the wattles on the neck are yellow. In New Guinea I have encountered five different varieties of scrub turkey.

BEGINNING AS A COLLECTOR

Regarding the crocodiles (sometimes wrongly called alligators) of North Queensland, there are some curious popular misconceptions. One is that the armour plating on the skin will protect the animal almost completely from rifle-bullets. As a matter of fact a crocodile skin is vulnerable at any point if the bullet strikes it directly, but the skin on the back of the creature is certainly strong enough to turn aside a glancing blow. Crocodiles are very common in the northern rivers of Australia and in most of the South Sea Islands.

I recollect at Rossel Island in the Louisiade group off the coast of New Guinea, hearing of and seeing a huge crocodile which the natives seemed to hold in a kind of veneration. They told the story that this crocodile used to bring supplies of turtle and fish for the villagers, and put these stores as food for them on a large ledge of rock. Certainly the crocodile did deposit these things as stated, but I suspect that it was not out of any love for the villagers. Possibly it might have had some connection with a habit which crocodiles are said to have, of keeping any prey they capture until it is in an advanced state of decomposition. I have heard that when the crocodile captures a calf or a human being, or any other prey of the kind, it is usual for it to hide the body away for some days before devouring it. Certainly the crocodile is a carrion feeder, and the effect of its bite, even when no actual serious wound has been inflicted, seems to be dangerous. Once at Fergusson Island, New Guinea, I was called to see a native who had been seized by a crocodile whilst fishing with nets from the shore. The man when he was seized by the crocodile cried out, and the other natives went to his assistance and managed to rescue him from the creature. When I was asked to see him two or three days had passed since he was wounded. The natives had the sick man on a platform with a fire smouldering underneath him so that the smoke should circle round him. All the wounds which he had received from the crocodile were suppurating badly and running with pus; this could be attributed to the infection of the crocodile's bite. I gave the natives some permanganate of potash to cleanse the sick man's wounds. He was all right afterwards.

At our camp on the Johnson River I got a great number of butterflies and birds, but the country did not offer many new things. The best bird of which we got specimens there was the Barnard Island Rifle Bird, also called the Victoria or Lesser Rifle Bird.[1] It is the smallest of the Australian Birds of Paradise.

We stayed on the Johnson River for some four months, without, as I have said, any very great

[1] The bird here mentioned by Mr. Meek is the *Ptilorhis victoriæ*, which is only found in North Queensland and on the Barnard Isles.—E. H.

BEGINNING AS A COLLECTOR

results, but still doing fairly well. I was able to make some interesting observations, however, of the habits of the Australian natives, who at that time in this district had not come very much into contact with white people. At Alligator Point, near our camp, there was a favourite meeting-place of the aboriginals, and some grand corroborees were held there. I have seen over 300 natives taking part in one of these. The natives were gorgeously painted up and were adorned with the down of young white cockatoos stuck with beeswax on to their bodies in geometrical designs. They carried shields of great size and also large clubs. The tactics in fighting seemed to be to try to beat down an enemy's guard with the club by mere brute force. The Kanakas engaged then on the sugar plantations would occasionally take part in the rows with the natives, and would use cross-cut saws in place of clubs.

The Australian aboriginals have no architecture, but a black fellow camping for a night usually makes a breakwind of bark, boughs or bushes on the side from which he expects the wind to blow during the night. His weather forecast is generally correct too. His bed is formed of green twigs or grass. Camps intended to be more permanent are usually bark huts open in front. In some places bark is almost exclusively used, and is good for the purpose, since it can be procured sometimes in slabs about twelve feet long and ten broad. Overhanging rocks, hollow trees and caves are sometimes used by the blacks, although caves are not in much favour because they are often credited with being haunted by evil spirits. When many natives happen to camp together, there are recognised camp rules. All boys and uninitiated young men sleep at a distance from the huts of the adults. Each inmate or family has a separate fire or several fires.

After we had exhausted the resources of the Johnson River, we decided to make a move on to the Bloomfield River. We chartered a small cutter to take us along the coast. The party at the time consisted of Barnard, myself, and an aboriginal boy named Tommy, who was very faithful to me and who turned out to be a very skilful collector.

On arrival at the Bloomfield River we found ourselves in country where the white man was almost unknown. The aboriginals were very numerous. We made a camp in a pocket of grass close to a jungle scrub seven miles to the north of the Bloomfield River. By this time I had abandoned the collection of mammals and confined my attention to lepidoptera and birds. One of the finest birds found there was the Pitta, of which I secured many specimens.[1] The aboriginals of the district were very clever with their spears, and could usually bring down a bird that was put up out of the scrub by a dog. I have seen

---

[1] This is the species known as *Pitta strepitans*.—E. H.

BEGINNING AS A COLLECTOR 35

one of the blacks get five or six scrub turkeys in succession whilst going through the scrub.

After staying on the Bloomfield River about three months we moved our camp to Cedar Bay, where we were the only white people and where I had the opportunity of observing the Australian aboriginal practically free from white interference. He is in my opinion a very good type of native, manly, plucky, honest, and truthful, though very lazy, except for work in which he happens to be interested. I have found Grey's observations on the Australian aborigines generally correct in my experience. The natives at Cedar Bay had exactly the equipment he describes as characteristic: " Round the man's middle is wound, in many folds, a cord spun from the fur of the opossum, forming a warm, soft and elastic belt of an inch in thickness, in which are stuck his stone hatchet, his boomerang, and a short heavy stick to throw at small animals. His hatchet is so placed, that the head of it rests exactly on the centre of his back, whilst its thin, short handle descends along the backbone. In his hand he carries his throwing stick, and several spears, headed in two or three different manners so that they are equally adapted to war or the chase. . . . The contents of the native woman's bag are : A flat stone to pound roots with; earth to mix with the pounded roots; quartz for the purpose of making spears and knives; stones for hatchets; prepared cakes of gum, to make and mend weapons and implements; kangaroo sinews to make spears and to sew with; needles made of the shin bones of kangaroos, with which they sew cloaks, bags, etc.; opossum hair to be spun into waist-belts; shavings of kangaroo skins to polish spears, etc.; the shell of a species of mussel to cut hair, etc. with; native knives; a native hatchet; pipe clay; red ochre, or burnt clay; yellow ochre; a piece of paper bark to carry water in; waist-bands and spare ornaments; banksia cones (small ones), or pieces of a dry white species of fungus, to kindle fire with rapidly, and to convey it from place to place; grease; the spare weapons of their husbands, or the pieces of wood from which these are to be manufactured; the roots, etc. which they have collected during the day. Skins not yet prepared for cloaks are generally carried between the bag and the back, so as to form a sort of cushion for the bag to rest on. In general each woman carries a lighted fire-stick, or brand, under her cloak and in her hand."

At this camp I managed to secure two clutches of the eggs of the rifle bird. A curious thing about the nest of the rifle bird is that the hen always seems to get a snake skin—the sloughed skin of a snake—to entwine in the fabric of her nest. I have encountered many nests of the rifle bird, and have always found a snake skin to be part of its fabric. The nests were usually built in the heads of the umbrella palms and

BEGINNING AS A COLLECTOR

were woven out of old vines. The eggs are of a pale pink with dark red and brown marks, striped longitudinally, as is the case with most eggs of Birds of Paradise.[1]

At Cedar Bay I discovered a male specimen of *Charagia mirabilis*, a new species of moth described by Mr. Rothschild. The male of this species has a strong, musk-like perfume. Another discovery made by me here was of a very beautiful moth, the hindwings rose-pink in colour, the fore-wings fawn-coloured with crimson spots bordered with white.[2]

We had some very good pig-shooting at this camp, and also some good sport hunting for sharks and for the dugong, that curious sea mammal which is said to have given rise to the story of the mermaid, because the female has breasts of a human type and has the habit of raising the fore-part of her body out of the water. But I have always failed to mistake a dugong for a mermaid.

The Australian natives are very fond of dugong flesh, which much resembles that of the pig in flavour. They hunt the animal industriously. They paddle out to him, and while he is under water lance him

---

[1] These eggs of the *Ptilorhis victoriæ* are among the most beautiful eggs. One of those collected by Mr. Meek is figured in the Tring Museum periodical called *Novitates Zoologicæ*, on Plate X, in Vol. XVII.—E. H.

[2] This is a very beautiful and large Pyral, representing a new species and new genus: *Hypsidia erythropsalis*, described by Mr. Rothschild in *Nov. Zool.*, p. 603 (1896).—K. J.

with a weapon which is curiously like the whale lance of the civilised man.

I stayed at Cedar Bay from June to Christmas, and then decided to make a trip home to England. That trip was I suppose the most perilous experience I have had during the whole course of my life. Our ship caught on fire and encountered terrible gales, and we were ten days overdue on our arrival.

I had now been away from England for five years, and was aged twenty-two. My purpose in coming to London was to see my people and to dispose of the collections I had made. But I was not at all tired of the life in the Antipodes. I think if it had been a question of going back to Australia and taking to " humping bluey " again I would cheerfully have gone rather than have faced the prospect of a city life. But, as it was, I was now getting into the stride of the work as a collector, and looked to the future with some degree of confidence.

I was not home long before I wanted to get away to the Bush again. So my stay in London on this occasion was limited to some three months. I saw the Hon. Walter Rothschild and made arrangements with him that I was to send all collections that I made to his Tring Museum and allow him the first choice of all specimens that I won. I had at the time formed no very definite plans as to my future movements, but I had decided to go either to New Guinea or West Australia collecting. What I desired was to explore new country where there was a chance of making some good discoveries. The western portion of Australia had been very little explored from a Natural History point of view at that time.

In 1894 I returned to Australia, having with me a man named Mr. Gulliver, whom I had known as a collector in the New Forest. At Rockhampton I picked up my old mate Mr. W. B. Barnard and also Mr. Harry Barnard, and we all went up to Cooktown. After full inquiry I had decided that New Guinea and the South Sea Islands offered better chances to the collector than West Australia. Cooktown was the best Australian seaport from which to set out for the islands. Thenceforth Cooktown was the only point of the civilised world with which I kept in close touch.

This collecting expedition was my venture solely, and the others were engaged by me as assistants. We outfitted at Cooktown and went on from there to Samarai, New Guinea, in the barquentine *Myrtle*. On the voyage across we met an Italian collector named Amido, who had been for a spell of six years in New Guinea, and I recollect many of the people on board thinking it a singular thing that he should still be alive. The reputation of the climate was very bad. The reputation of the natives was worse. I have now been in all some eighteen years in New Guinea and the Solomons, and do not consider it impossible to live there fifty years if one is reasonably careful. The average idea about New Guinea and other tropical places is that the climate is worse and the natives more savage than they really are. But one must have some rules of life.

As regards the climate, to take with one a stock of whisky or any other spirits is to invite trouble and to have the invitation promptly accepted. Possibly some people can take alcohol in moderation in tropical climates without serious harm to their health. But the trouble is that when out in the wilderness, lonely and without distraction, moderation soon drifts into immoderation. It is extremely difficult to be a strictly moderate drinker when you are the only white man in a forest camp or a trading hut, a week's journey from the next white man. The safest course is to have no supply of alcohol at all, except what may be carried as medicine and used only as medicine.

Apart from caution in regard to alcohol I think that the most necessary thing in the tropics is to take a great deal of exercise. The chance of a lazy life of course never came my way, so that I was never tempted to loaf. But I have seen enough to conclude that it is the man who is afraid to sweat whose liver hardens or who falls ill in a tropical climate. An exaggerated fear of the sun causes more illness than it wards off.

On my first voyage to New Guinea I had still practically everything to learn in regard to the customs of the country and the precautions which it was necessary to take against disease. But now after many years' experience I find that no very elaborate preparations are necessary for a six months' dive into the New Guinea forest. I take ordinary stores of food, quinine as a remedy against fever, a little brandy for medical use if that is feasible, and my drug-case contains Epsom Salts, permanganate of potash, and chlorodyne. The most serious part of my outfitting equipment is that which is needed for the collections which I make. The butterfly hunter who contemplates a six months' plunge into virgin forest must carry a collecting outfit not differing much in character from that of a naturalist putting in a week-end in the New Forest. But he must enormously increase the quantity of his gear, and if his work is to be, as mine was, in a damp, tropical climate some special precautions are needed against mildew. On the expedition in which I am to be engaged this year (1913) I shall take a good supply of butterfly nets—sufficient for the use of the collecting boys I directly employ, and of friendly natives who can be enlisted temporarily as collectors; a supply of non-rusting pins for setting; killing-bottles with cyanide of potassium for killing small insects and syringes with acetic acid for killing large insects; pill-boxes for small insects; japanned tin air-tight and cork-lined collecting cases. It is simple enough on paper; not so simple when it has to be carried strung on poles by bearers through the mountain jungles.

CHAPTER III

MY FIRST EXPEDITION TO NEW GUINEA

THE impression on the traveller of the first sight of the South Sea Islands remains always in the memory. One seems to have strayed into the land of the fairy books. The intensely blue water foaming to a dazzling white against the coral reefs; the sharp outlines of the hills covered with trees of such strange but regular shapes that they seem like temples made by man; the gay colouring of the natives—bronze of skin, their hair often dyed a brilliant red, their dazzling white teeth showing in a perpetual smile—all seem to be too pretty to be real.

We had reached near to the port of Samarai at night-time and had anchored outside the reef until the dawn. Coming on deck in the morning I found that our vessel had been brought inside the reef, and we were surrounded by little islands covered with coco-nut palms and tropical jungle. It was August, and a bright winter day. Everything was glowing with colour and light. The natives surrounded our vessel, chattering eagerly and offering to trade. They had stores of coco-nuts, of dried fish, of bêche-de-mer (the sea-slug which makes such excellent soup), of

MY FIRST EXPEDITION TO NEW GUINEA

tropical fruit and of flowers. In return for their goods they wanted tobacco or any article of steel.

The natives of New Guinea at that time were much less used to the white man than they are now, and perhaps there will be some interest in the first observations I made of an interesting people, whose native ways and customs are now gradually being lost through contact with whites.

The Papuan men of the coast in their native state dress in a short trunk around the loins made of pandanus leaf. This leaf the natives pick when it is green, and mark it with a sharp shell in some pretty design. The leaf is then run over a fire and finally dried in the sun, becoming after this soft and pliable. Two leaves suffice for a man's wardrobe. They are tied around his waist with string made of a vine which is interlaced with the yellow skin of the stem of an orchid. Both in the marking of the pandanus leaf and in the plaiting of the string there is evidence of some artistic feeling. What I have said applies to the natives round Samarai. On the north coast the waist-belt is usually of interlaced human hair. The New Guinea native carries his purse on his arm in the shape of armlets of native shell-money. He ordinarily wears his hair bleached to a Titian red colour with lime and frizzed out with combs.

The Papuan women-folk usually wear a short petticoat woven of the young leaves of the coco-nut or of the sago palm. The leaves of the sago palm make the better cloth. This cloth is stained in artistic designs with different colours, red, yellow, or grey. A petticoat reaching from the waist half-way down the thighs is the ordinary dress of the women. But when a woman is with child she will often wear a shawl of native cloth over her shoulder, and this drapes her whole body.

At Samarai I put up at a trader's house and got into touch with Mr. Whitton, the chief trader there, learning from him the best part of the coast to go to in order to penetrate to the inland mountains. My idea was to explore the mountains for lepidoptera. Mr. Whitton advised me to go along the North-East Coast to Fergusson Island. There the mountains came close to the coast. Accordingly I chartered a cutter called the *Pioneer*, a vessel of six tons, with a native crew of five, and we made our way to Fergusson Island. The coast natives of New Guinea are as a rule very good sailors, and a great deal of the trade of the South Sea Islands is carried on with their help.

We had a fine trip lasting for three or four days, with a strong trade wind blowing by day and dying away by night. Navigation in the South Sea Islands is made easy usually by the regularity of the winds. Hurricanes are rare. The trade wind, which reaches its greatest strength by day and fades away at night, is a great convenience, for it is usual to anchor during the night in the shelter of some island or reef and to voyage only by daylight.

SAMARAI, PAPUAN MAINLAND IN DISTANCE.

POLICE MAGISTRATE'S HOUSE, SAMARAI.

MY FIRST EXPEDITION TO NEW GUINEA

At Fergusson Island I picked upon a spot near the village of Nadi as my first camping-ground. There was there a Kanaka named Harry, who had been employed on the Queensland sugar plantations and knew how to speak English. He was a New Hebrides boy and was engaged in trading in copra. He proved to be very obliging and helped me considerably with the natives. In a very short while there was put up a fine house for us in the native style, with a broad deep verandah. This I made my headquarters, and from there sent my men out collecting. I had my three white assistants, and the natives also brought in great quantities of beetles and birds and also some mammals.

Our native house was built of saplings with a roof of matted sago palm leaves. A native house of that sort is very comfortable and will last, say, six or twelve months. Then the weevil gets into the sago leaves and eats the roof away, and the white ant attacks the timber, and your house very quickly crumbles. When the natives are building houses for themselves they can often make them so that they will last some five years, by matting the leaves very thickly and building the roofs with a very high pitch. Also they keep fires going constantly in the houses, and the smoke percolating through keeps down the ravages of insects.

There is a great diversity of opinion among white residents in New Guinea regarding the advantages and disadvantages of the native houses. Some of the Government officials abuse the native houses very cordially, saying that the roofs are not watertight, that they harbour vermin, and so on; and make a demand for iron roofs. Galvanised iron is thus coming into vogue as a roofing material in New Guinea. It is hideously ugly, makes a house uncomfortably hot, and has but one advantage, that the rain-water collected from it is of good quality. From my experience I prefer the native house and the native style of roofing, but it must be constructed properly. A scamped roof of sago leaves of course will leak; but a properly thatched one will not, and it will keep out the heat of the sun as well as the rain. A native house must be renewed frequently, of course. But that is rather an advantage than otherwise. The old house can be burned down and all its germs will perish with it. On the other hand houses of wood and iron, however carefully they are kept clean, will in time become harbouring grounds for the germs of tropical diseases. My vote is for the well-built native house (with some European improvements), often renewed like the lamb in the "happy family" of a menagerie.

At Nadi I made a very fine collection and discovered several new birds, including a new parrot and a new podargus ("mopoke" is the Australian name). Also I discovered a great number of new day-flying moths with very beautiful antennæ. I do not know exactly

A GAOLER, SAMARAI.

BOAT BOYS, PAPUA.

To face p. 46.

MY FIRST EXPEDITION TO NEW GUINEA

why these are called "day-flying moths," because in my experience they have to be beaten out of the undergrowth, and are not to be discovered flying about in the daytime. The popular division of butterflies and moths into two classes of lepidoptera, one of which flies by day and the other by night, one of which is bright-coloured and the other dull-coloured, is not at all correct. There are some moths which fly by day and some which are very bright-coloured, and there are some butterflies which only fly by night.

Whilst I had been in Northern Australia I had encountered that great enemy of the white man in the tropics, malarial fever, but my experience of it had been of comparatively trifling inconvenience. Here at Nadi I had been established only three weeks when I suffered from a very severe attack of malaria. Since then, all the time that I have been in New Guinea, I have been subject to attacks of this fever, but I am at least counted to be lucky in that I never suffer from it when I am away from the South Sea Islands. But the first hard attack of malarial fever was very disquieting. Shivering fits were followed by fits of sleepiness. At one moment it was impossible to get warm, at another moment the skin seemed to be burning, as if one were being roasted in a fire. A terrible thirst would be followed by severe nausea. Then finally a sweating fit would mark the end of an attack, but there would follow sometimes severe headache and great weakness.

At Nadi the fever troubled me more than at any time since in New Guinea. I recollect during one attack that I had the strange fancy that I was five different people with five different personalities, all doing different things at the same time. At one time I seemed to be threatened with death. But in time I got better, and afterwards I seemed to be somewhat hardened to the fever.

During the time I was at Nadi I ate about the same kinds of food that I was accustomed to in Australia, using tinned provisions mostly; but the natives supplemented those provisions with taro, yams, sweet potatoes, sago, and coco-nuts. I never used alcohol except for medicinal purposes. I found that a little brandy taken when the first shivering fit came on would sometimes stave off, or nip in the bud, an attack of fever. At this time I did not smoke, though I had with me a large quantity of trade tobacco, which was the common currency of the time for dealing with the natives. Tobacco was rare on the coast then. The natives smoked it in bamboo pipes somewhat similar to the pipes which the Chinese use for smoking opium. Smoking a pipe was quite an elaborate ceremony. The native who was happy enough to be the possessor of a little bit of tobacco would roll it with a green leaf into a kind of cigarette. This would be inserted in a hole in the bamboo pipe and the smoker would then hold to the tobacco a live coal and deeply inhale the smoke. Then the pipe

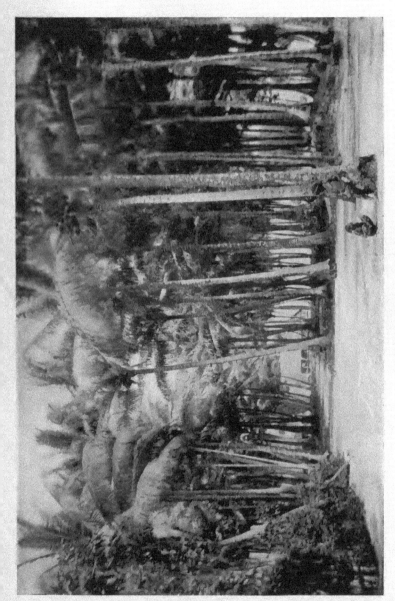

GOVERNMENT QUARTERS, SAMARAI.

MY FIRST EXPEDITION TO NEW GUINEA 49

would be passed round to his friends. The idea was to get the full narcotic value of the tobacco. Nowadays the progress of civilisation has brought cigarettes within easy reach of most Papuans, and a native smoking a pipe is rarely to be encountered.

It was at Nadi that I encountered for the first time a true Bird of Paradise, that variety which is called the grey-breasted Bird of Paradise.[1] The natives of New Guinea are able to imitate the call of the Bird of Paradise to its mates and thus will lure specimens for the hunter. In my observations of the different species of the true *Paradisea* (which has extended over some years), I have never known an instance where two kinds of the *true Paradisea* are to be found in one district. Each particular kind seems to have its own district. Sometimes, however, between one district and another, on the borderland, you may get an intermediate species, having some of the characteristics of the particular birds of the two districts.

My chief aim, however, in collecting was insects, and not birds. As this was my first collecting trip in New Guinea I was still lacking somewhat in experience, and I cannot chronicle anything really big in the way of a discovery, but I was getting valuable training as to the ways of the natives and the best manner of working with them. One of the things that

---

[1] This is the rare *Paradisea decora*, which is entirely restricted to the islands of the D'Entrecasteaux group, and perhaps only to the Fergusson island.—E. H.

I soon learnt was that it is best to take them from their home district to another district if you want to get good work. They are far more reliable when they are away from home. The difficulties of getting native labour in New Guinea are now very quickly increasing. Wherever the white man has taken up his dwelling the natives have become possessed of such of the white possessions as they need, and it is difficult then to get them to work. Any one wishing to get reliable native workmen in the South Sea Islands nowadays always tries to tap a district where the natives are unaccustomed to white men. Very soon after the white men come to a place to settle, the natives get as much of white " trade " as they wish— a little cloth, steel, mirrors, and the like. Having obtained these, they feel very little of that pressure which drives the people of civilised lands to work in order that they may live. The South Sea Islander can live with very little work indeed, and altogether without the work which the white man wants done.

Some of the white officials in New Guinea—mostly those by the way who know most closely the coastal districts—consider that there is a real " economic pressure " on the natives. Thus a well-known resident magistrate reported to his Government last year:—

" Statements are at times made that natives exist in comparative luxury in their own villages without doing any work. But this can hardly be true generally. The native must eat and he can only get

MY FIRST EXPEDITION TO NEW GUINEA 51

food from his garden if he has cleared the ground, and kept wild pigs away by a fence or by guarding the garden. If he has tobacco, either he or his fellow-villagers must have worked for it. If he wants meat he must hunt for it. If he wants a house he must build it, and native houses require continual repairs if they are to be kept dry and in reasonable repair, or reasonably comfortable even from the natives' point of view. As in every other place there will always be a certain proportion of the population idle at any one moment; and if Europeans visit at all unfrequented villages the entire village not unusually stays at home to see them, and of course the visitor finds them all 'doing nothing.' If, however, a native 'goes to work' he is more certain of regular food and perhaps of better quarters. On the other hand, he is entering on the unknown and may find himself at the mercy of an unsympathetic 'boss,' whom he can neither understand, nor who can understand him. In any case there is the loss of the sense of freedom which a village native must feel. The dysentery epidemics have also carried off some hundreds of natives, and this cannot but discourage the others from going to work. Another aspect of the question is perhaps sometimes lost sight of. The recognised cost of feeding and clothing a native amounts to about £7 a year. This includes only actual food consumed, 1 lb. only of meat per week, one blanket, and four sulus; it does not allow for the cost of a house or of any luxuries beyond a stick of tobacco a week. The cost to a native of keeping a wife can hardly be less than this; but his wages, as a rule, only amount to £6 a year. In other words, it is very difficult to see how a native can in Papua support a wife and family on his ordinary wage. It may well be that his wife can *at times* earn something for herself, and it may be that *at places* she can buy native food cheaply; but I believe the general experience is that in the end it is cheaper and more economical to buy rice rather than plant native food. The decisive factor in inducing a native to leave his home the first time for work is, I believe, a desire to see more of the world, with at times the hope of earning sufficient wealth to buy a wife. These factors act with less effect a second time a native is asked to go to work.

"It is certainly a great inducement to a native to go to work if he knows definitely where he is going to work, if he knows from direct information given him by his own relatives and friends that it is a comfortable place, if he knows that he will always have some one of his own friends whom he can look to be his leader and who is capable of stating his case to his employer if he should have any grievances, and if his immediate employer will listen to and deal sympathetically with any grievances which may arise. If these conditions are met I see no reason why natives should not be supplied continuously for work on the plantations in the near future."

A HOUSE PARTLY EUROPEAN, PARTLY PAPUAN IN STYLE.

MY FIRST EXPEDITION TO NEW GUINEA

That is an optimistic view, which I believe is partly shared by his Excellency the Administrator. If it is fully justified, then the recent attempt to pass a Labour Ordinance compelling the Papuan natives to do a certain small amount of work was not unwisely vetoed by the Australian Parliament. But the opinion I have formed from my travels in New Guinea is that, except in the first greed for the white man's "trade," a greed which soon passes, the natives will not work in the steady fashion which civilised enterprises demand, unless some slight compulsion is enforced.

At that time at Nadi all the natives had skulls hung up as adornments for the gables of their huts. These were trophies of the old days when head-hunting was permitted. Now of course head-hunting is forbidden by the British authorities, but occasionally in my time tribes used to come down from the Bush to attack the coast natives and carry off a few of them. I did not notice that the New Guinea natives at that time set any very great value on the human skulls that they had collected. Once I was able to purchase three for a single stick of tobacco. But in the Solomon Islands the natives set a very great value on their human skulls, and will hardly part from them at any price. In New Guinea they seemed to be accounted just like ordinary trophies of the chase, of the same value as turtles' heads, or the lower jaw of pigs.

There was no open practice of cannibalism when I first reached New Guinea, and I cannot say that I have had any proved cases coming under my notice, though it is of course practised. I noticed indeed in the last criminal report of the Papuan Administration that there had been one or two cases of cannibalism proved among the natives and punished. The horror with which cannibalism is viewed in this country does not seem to me to be justified by my observation of its effects on savages. Roughly speaking the savage who is a cannibal is not necessarily a degraded type. In fact with the savages I have known, as a rule, those who had practised cannibalism were of a better type than those who had not. I do not wish to argue from this that cannibalism is a means of raising the status of the savage; but it certainly seems to have no degrading effect.

I never had any great cause for fear in dealing with the New Guinea natives. In my experience they are a great deal afraid of the white man, and would rarely molest him unless they were interfered with first. The guiding principle in dealing with them, as I think it is with most savages, is not to get excited or flurried. So long as you keep your nerve and your temper you have little or nothing to fear. I have been of course, at different times, in positions which seemed to suggest great peril, but with calmness and with firmness the most difficult position soon relieved itself. The most serious troubles I have had in

New Guinea were when I have approached some inland village with my train of bearers from the coast, and have been refused permission to proceed. Sometimes I have had to make this concession to the hill natives: to send back my coast bearers and to go forward alone and get fresh bearers from the country through which I was going to pass. But I have never had to use mortal violence on the natives. I think the only killing I ever had to do was to shoot a venerable pig belonging to a village where the white man was quite unknown. This was as a sign that firearms were powerful, and it had its effect.

But probably that has been my good fortune rather than my good management. There have been occasions when it seemed for a while that bloodshed was the only way out of a difficulty. And I know that the government officials, who in all cases are very anxious to treat the natives as gently as possible, sometimes find it necessary to use firearms. Only recently, in connection with one of the expeditions which had been sent out to search for Mr. Stanniforth Smith—who had gone on an inland exploration trip and had lost his way—a tragedy occurred. The officer's own report of the incident was :—

"We saw no natives until we were within three days of the Ilo, when we came across a small party making sago, and with whom we made friends. From their manner of receiving us I feel sure that these people had never seen white men before. From there to the Ilo we saw a good number of natives, with whom we made friends. The Ilo natives came to meet us and escorted us through their country. A most regrettable tragedy occurred on our arrival at the Ilo. We had pulled up on a stony beach on the banks of a stream to give the carriers a spell and a smoke. We were surrounded by about fifty natives, all, apparently, most friendly; they informed us by signs to wait and they would bring us a pig. I had promised one of the natives a knife. In giving it to him I noticed that he was very excited, and also that they all appeared more or less excited, so I decided to move on. I drew the attention of Evans and Stanton to the state of affairs, and told them to look out. I felt sure that the natives were going to make an attack on us, but thought it would be in the form of a shower of arrows. I told the carriers to make a move, and they were about to do so when one of the natives grabbed one of them by the hair and smashed in his skull with a stone club; other natives were holding some of our carriers. Stanton saw the native in the act of striking the fatal blow and fired at him, but, unfortunately, not in time to prevent the catastrophe.

" In self-defence we had to fire on them, and, when it was over, there were two dead natives, and one dying and unconscious carrier on the ground. The whole thing did not last more than half a minute; no doubt they had intended to try to get the lot of us, but their hearts failed them and their plans fell through. This occurred at about 4 p.m.

"I made a stretcher and had our dying carrier carried on about half-a-mile, where we camped for the night. The carrier died that evening, and we buried him next morning. We saw nothing more of the natives. Our carriers were very frightened and most of them spent a sleepless night. These natives are a fine type of men; light-coloured, and averaging about five feet four inches in height, and strongly built. Their weapons consist of bows and arrows, and a small stone disc club, and for ornaments they wore dried human hands, cassowary plumes, land shells, and seed necklaces."

Now that, I should say, was a case of sheer bad luck. Probably the attacking natives had their cupidity aroused by seeing some of the "trade" of the exploring party; and were ignorant of the power of the white man's arms. If they had been kept at a distance until they had seen the effects of a gunshot on a pig or some other animal, probably they would not have dared to meddle.

The coast people in New Guinea as a rule are great thieves. The hill people on the other hand are fairly honest. After contact with white people the natives generally become less honest. Sometimes their dishonesty is so naïve as to be amusing. They will come and steal things from your camp and openly wear them as ornaments, and after you have bought curios from them and stored them, they will steal them and bring them back to you to sell again.

After staying at Nadi for some four months I went across to Cooktown, partly to dispatch my collections to Europe and partly because I was beginning to be somewhat alarmed about the fits of fever from which I suffered. I went as far as Samarai from Nadi in the cutter *Mizpah*, a little vessel which had a tragic history afterwards. It was stolen from Samarai by two Germans, who took it to New Britain, where the natives captured the boat, killed one of the Germans and took the other prisoner and kept him as a slave. The Germans in stealing the boat had had the idea of "living among the natives." The one who survived had more experience of living among the natives than he cared for. They kept him in a kind of slavery, and whenever a Government boat came near their village they would truss him up on a pole and take him into the jungle. Finally the Germans heard about a white man being kept in the village and sent an expedition to recover him. I think he was cured of his desire to "live among the natives."

Probably the idea of the natives in keeping him as a prisoner was that he would be useful as a "magic" worker. All the life of the natives of the South Sea Islands is coloured by a belief in sorcery. Usually the sorcerer is some fellow with more brains and less industry than his fellows who pretends to be a "magic man." In a more civilised state of life I suppose he would become a Member of Parliament and, as such, do great good to his fellow-men. In the South Seas the only way that he can win to authority and respect is by pretending to have powers as a sorcerer. He casts the "evil eye" on those who question his authority or resist his exactions, and—such is the effect of mental suggestion on bodily conditions—the victim of the sorcerer will often die from sheer funk.

Quite the most amusing instance of a sorcerer's impudence that I have heard of is on official record, having recently come before a native magistrate's court. An old policeman, named Tai-imi, profiting by what his police experience had taught him, had set up practice as a sorcerer on the Gira River. He had his snakes, invisible to ordinary eyes, but nevertheless very deadly and real to any who obtained the ill-will of the sorcerer. To enhance his dignity, Tai-imi chose five minor sorcerers to assist him. One he created "sergeant," and another "corporal." The remaining three were "orderlies"; their duties were to cook for and attend to the wants of Tai-imi and his officers. The sergeant was endowed with a snake similar to the one possessed by Tai-imi; the corporal was also given one, but smaller, and the three orderlies were promised snakes should their loyalty merit such a reward. Every day when Tai-imi started his rounds his company fell in in the centre of the village, and saluted him in military fashion. Tai-imi returned the salute, and inspected the company. Presently, everybody in the village was saluting him; from them it spread to other villages. The village constables on the Gira thought it better to fall in with the prevailing custom, and they commenced to salute; if they did not, they were arraigned before Tai-imi, and threatened with a visit from the snake. In the meantime, Tai-imi's appetite for pigs was growing and the victims began to murmur. They complained to the Government, and this amusing scoundrel was brought to heel and sent as a prisoner to work on the roads. Probably when he has finished his term as prisoner he will become a constable again. Very many of the native constabulary are recruited from prisoners who have served their sentences, and whilst serving them have come to a useful knowledge of the white man's wants. In fact there is a large proportion of murderers in the Papuan police force: and excellent law-abiding policemen they make. Murder among the natives, of course, is not treated as a serious crime. Its punishment is anything from eighteen months' imprisonment to "discharged on his own recognisances." Pretending to exercise sorcery is quite as serious an offence in the eyes of the white law.

Having reached Samarai in the *Mizpah* I went from Samarai to Cooktown in the trading schooner *Myrtle*, encountering very heavy weather owing to the north-west monsoon. The voyage occupied thirteen days. I had no intention, in spite of the

MY FIRST EXPEDITION TO NEW GUINEA

fever, of abandoning New Guinea, and before I left Nadi I had made arrangements for my camp to be shifted to the Trobriand Islands. When I arrived at Cooktown I was very ill and found it difficult for some time to take any nourishment, but still I only remained there sufficiently long to send on my collections to the Hon. Walter Rothschild, and then I took the *Myrtle* back to Samarai.

CHAPTER IV

A TRIP TO THE TROBRIANDS

HAVING completed my outfit at Samarai I went straight on to the Trobriand Islands in a little boat called the *Fleet Wing*. I hoped there to explore some " new " territory in the Natural History sense. This was my first experience of the natives of the Trobriands. They are, I think, without exception the most immoral in the South Seas. At this time (1895) at any rate that would apply. Since then the efforts of the Government and of the missionaries have effected some change. Before the coming of the white man the natives of the Trobriands seemed to have had an exceptionally low moral standard. Nevertheless they are of a bright engaging type, softer in their manners than most of the Papuans, slightly taller, lighter in colour, not honest in trading, with no notion at all of truth, and little of morality.

I found that my boys had followed my instructions, and my camp had been moved from Nadi and established at the Trobriands in good order. We started at once to collect birds and insects. I made here a very interesting discovery in obtaining quite a series of specimens of a fine new moth allied to *Charagia mirabilis,* of which I had found a single male at Cedar Bay in Queensland.[1]

I stayed at the Trobriands during March, April, May, June, and July, the winter season, when the weather was fine, cool, and pleasant, but I had the misfortune there to lose Mr. Gulliver, whom I had brought with me from England. The tropical life did not suit him at all. He was not able to take quinine to ward off the fever. When I reached the Trobriands from Samarai I found him very ill and sent him back to Samarai in the *Fleet Wing.* He died there. I was sorry to lose him, for he had been a good and conscientious worker.

I did not find the Trobriands as good for collecting as Nadi. These islands were not so rich in insect life, but I had hopes of getting some new things and so stayed on there. The natives used to help willingly in collecting and I got on very well with them on the whole. I recollect an encounter one evening with the natives, showing their good temper if they are treated firmly and kindly. I had designed to take a trip by moonlight across the island on which we were camped and had engaged two boys to show me the road across. After we had left the coast behind some distance, we came upon three inland villages built very close together. All the villagers were asleep. I passed

---

[1] *Charagia marginatus,* Rothschild, *Nov. Zool.,* 1896, p. 326. Mr. Meek collected both sexes of this species.—K. J.

through the first without making any noise, but in the second village some of the sleepers were aroused, and followed us, full of curiosity mingled with alarm.

The third village was aroused thoroughly before we entered it, and there were over 1000 people collected in the main street. Apparently they did not wish us any harm, but were anxious that we should stop in the village to answer their inquiries, and they offered us food and presents. I wanted to push on, but the natives seemed to think that this was an unfriendly attitude on my part. Trouble was apparently brewing. Finally I was struck by something that a child had thrown, but of course did not retaliate. Then a man who was in mourning for some dead relative and was covered over with black pigment, as is the custom there, put his hand on my white clothes, soiling them badly. At the same time he pushed me. I knocked him over and the natives then dispersed a little. My boys were very frightened, but they followed me as I pushed on, the natives following behind with spears. Their attitude was so threatening that I thought it best to halt and parley with them. I tried the effect of fear, firing my revolver at a tree. They had evidently never heard firearms before and some of them fell to the ground in fright. I gave two or three of the men some tobacco, and then they seemed friendly enough and allowed me to pass on.

During the night we passed through several large

SCENE, TROBRIAND ISLANDS.

To face p. 64.

TROBRIANDER MAKING FISHING NETS.

CHIEF'S HOUSE, TROBRIANDS.

A TRIP TO THE TROBRIANDS

villages, but I took every possible care to prevent the inhabitants from being aroused. It was not that the natives were hostile, but they were curious and wanted the white man to stop. Others of them were very frightened. My coming was like that of a hawk to a poultry-yard.

Agriculture in the Trobriands is very flourishing. At the time of my first visit all the villages were surrounded by large gardens of taro and yams. Contact with the white man since has not spoiled the love of the natives for their primitive industry. The 1911 Government report on the Trobriands states—

"The Trobriand native is by birth and education an agriculturist. He is a pearl-diver rather by accident than from choice. The pearling is confined to the villages which dot the coast-line of the bay. Outside these bay villages, the topic of interest, the centre of social gravity, and the fulcrum of family and tribal prosperity is the garden. I know of no other place in Papua, either island or mainland, where the idle man is held up to such ridicule as he is in the Trobriand Group. Here it is impossible for an idle man, that is, a man without gardens, to marry. No parents will give their girl to a man who has little or no garden. The garden is the measure of a man's wealth. Yams, taitu, taro, sugar-cane, bananas, and sweet potatoes; they grow them all, and sell the surplus. Last year about 300 tons were produced above their own requirements. This was either bought locally by the Government for the use of the station here, by the Methodist Mission, or by the traders for export to Samarai, Milne Bay, or Woodlark Island."

I was interested in noticing the great precautions the Trobrianders took to guard their gardens from wild pigs, setting sharpened stakes in the ground so that were a wild pig to break through a gap in the fence he would become impaled on the stakes. They had also a sort of bell made of a shell with a stone inside, which hung on branches and gave warning to the gardener of the passage of any animal into his grounds.

The big chief of the Trobriands at that time was named Enumakali. He had thirty-six wives and occupied a village all to himself. The other villages around paid to him tribute. Whenever he went on a voyage travellers ran before him to give warning to the villages, and in any village he was going to visit a stage was set up. There he would stop and hold a council. The natives would crouch before him when they approached his presence. This ceremonial still survives in the Trobriands, and the British authorities had amusing trouble the other day when they had to put a Trobriand chief named Toulu into gaol for practising sorcery.

There were about a dozen other prisoners in gaol at the time. " I was considerably surprised " (records the magistrate for the district), " on visiting the gang

YAM HOUSES, TROBRIANDS.

A TRIP TO THE TROBRIANDS

the morning of Toulu's arrival to find them all working in a huddled-up position. No man can use a crowbar properly lying on his stomach. I have a suspicion that the prison warder was bending at the moment of my approach. He, however, professed to be looking for something on the ground. I told Toulu that ceremonial must be in abeyance until he was discharged. He said nothing, but the expression of his face said, ' It is your fault for putting me here.' The other prisoners straightened themselves with relief, but, half-an-hour later, on looking furtively round a corner, I saw that they were all on their stomachs again. The gaoler had compromised with a Gibson Girl bend. I have an idea that any prisoner showing a tendency to straighten himself got a glare from Toulu and straightway fell to his crouching position again. Thenceforward, Toulu worked by himself, and not with the regular gang."

The chief Enumakali was always surrounded with fighting men who had spears and clubs of ebony. If any one wanted a big canoe to travel any great voyage by sea it was necessary to ask him first for permission to take the war vessel. His sway ruled over many of the Trobriand Islands.

The children of the Trobrianders are very intelligent and the women engaging in appearance, but quite deficient in any moral sense. It seemed to be the custom among them to indulge their passions quite freely and almost promiscuously until they were married. Then some degree of fidelity is insisted upon by the husband. There are never any children born of these illicit love affairs: but the marriages are usually fruitful. The women evidently have means of preventing conception when they wish. The general looseness of morals among the Trobrianders is reflected in their religious rites, which seem to be chiefly inspired by phallic worship.

The architecture of the Trobrianders is fairly good, and a noticeable thing is the large storehouses they build for the storage of yams. Agriculture is so flourishing that sometimes a single garden of a village will extend for half a mile. The natives are not good sailors but they are great fishermen, and are accustomed to keep a watchman posted on a look-out for shoals of fish coming within the reefs. When a shoal of mullet had come within the reef the watchman would give warning, and men posted along the road from the beach to the villages (which were mostly inland) would carry the warning along. Within ten minutes of the fish being noticed the people of the village would have their nets ready and be rushing for the beach.

The method of fishing was to surround the shoal of fish with nets held on rods in such a way as to form a fence around the shoal. These nets would then be gradually pushed in, forcing the fish to crowd together. The result would be that the fish would leap up into the air. As they jumped they would be captured in

NATIVE GIRLS, TROBRIANDS.

small hand-nets set on poles, constructed on very much the same principle as butterfly nets. The fish are always eaten fresh and the natives seem to have no way of preserving them.

The " medicine man " or sorcerer came a great deal under my notice in the Trobriands. The sorcerer is a man of evil over all the South Seas. Ordinarily, a native with more brains and less principles than the average, he finds that a lazy and well-fed existence is obtainable by pretending to exercise powers of magic. These sorcerers are very much like the medical quacks of civilised peoples, and their great art consists of inventing imaginary diseases and thus frightening people into sickness. All over the South Seas the barb of the stingaree is used by the medicine man as " magic." In my early days in the South Seas the sorcerers did not profess to have any power over the white man, but lately their impudence seems to be growing, and a medicine man will sometimes pretend that he has cast the evil eye on a white man. Usually he waits until the white man is sickening of some fever and then he pretends that his " magic " is the cause of that illness.

A steady campaign is carried on by the Australian Government officials against the practice of sorcery; but it seems doubtful whether it has very much effect. At any rate I notice that last year the Resident Magistrate in one district had to record no less than 174 cases of sorcery. His narrative of how these cases came before him will give a very good idea of the ways of the sorcery man in Papua :

"The number of sorcery cases will at once attract attention as remarkable. It does not, however, indicate any widespread growth of sorcery or even any unusual energy on the part of the village police or the magistrate to root out this offence. The largest tribe in the Division, the Maisin people, were perturbed at the number of deaths in their villages, and came to the conclusion that the deaths must be due to the sorcery experts among their friends the Kubiri people. They decided that this could not be allowed to go on without making the Kubiri people pay for it. So the Maisin natives to the number of seventy-one went to the Kubiri villages and said, ' You must pay for these people you have killed '—fortunately the Papuan will usually accept a pig as compensation for any relative, especially if the Government is near—' or else our sorcerers will make pouri-pouri and take payment by making all sorts of disasters happen to your tribe.' The Kubiri people promptly handed over the required pigs and other articles, more apparently from fear of pouri-pouri than from fear of any actual violence. News was shortly brought to the Government station and a summons sent to the Maisin people to come in. This they did to the number of sixty-five, and the six stragglers arrived during the next few days and explained that they were away from the village when the summons came. They all

VILLAGE, TROBRIANDS.

ALBINO CHILD, TROBRIANDS.

A TRIP TO THE TROBRIANDS

candidly admitted the facts. The leaders were sent to gaol for three months, and the others for one month. The incident would be of comparatively little importance were it not for the underlying fact that the offence was nothing more than a symptom of the number of deaths which have occurred in the settled parts of the Division during the last few years. These deaths are all put down to sorcery and payment sought in the usual way. It may be that the friends of the deceased make pouri-pouri to kill the supposed murderer. It may be that they demand pigs; it may be that they attempt to square matters by killing the supposed sorcerer or a relative; or it may be that they come to the magistrate and want to lay a complaint for murder.

" Sorcery is probably widespread in the Division, but the fear of sorcery without due cause probably does far more harm than the sorcerers do either directly or indirectly by causing fear. In common with pretty well all races in a low degree of culture the Papuan is surrounded by natural processes he does not understand, but which he vainly, although quite honestly, believes he can control—at least if a more expert sorcerer does not thwart him. He sees a friend die —it may be of pneumonia—but the fact is proof positive to him that some one has murdered him by magical means. If he wants rain to come he has only to apply to the nearest rain-maker, who puts the appropriate articles in a stream of water and perhaps recites the appropriate spells, and in this wet part of the Territory rain is pretty sure to come before very long. If a plentiful supply of garden produce is required there is probably some one who knows the right article to bury in the garden, etc. A short time ago two police were sent in a canoe along the coast. They came back after some slight delay very indignant with one another. One complained that he had arrested and handcuffed a native and that the other one had promptly released him. It appears that they were delayed at Pongani by rough weather, so the more courageous of the two decided to arrest the local storm-maker, and did so. The other policeman when asked to explain why he had ventured to release a man under arrest explained—not that he had grown out of such beliefs but that he only released the storm-maker because he was afraid that if the storm-maker was kept under arrest he would naturally keep the sea rough, and perhaps prevent them from getting back altogether."

As collecting work at the Trobriands was not proving very profitable I chartered a schooner, the *Ellen Gowan,* to take me to Woodlark Island with the two Barnards. Woodlark Island was then very little known to the white man and was comparatively isolated. I hoped to get some good specimens there. This was just at the time of the first of the gold discoveries. On our way to Woodlark Island we called in at the Egham Islands. The natives of the

PREPARING FOR A FEAST, TROBRIANDS.

YAM STORES, TROBRIANDS.

Egham Islands are great sailors and skilled makers of sailing canoes. They have in their hands almost all the trade between Woodlark Island and the Trobriands.

When we arrived at Woodlark Island I lost one of my staff, as Mr. Tim Barnard found that fever and rheumatism were afflicting him so badly that it was necessary to return to Queensland. We camped at Suloya and at once I began collecting, to which I added a little trading. At Woodlark Island one gets that form of money very much prized in the South Seas, called "tomahawk stones." The tomahawk stones are made of a kind of dark jade. The natives of Woodlark Island quarry this out of the earth with the aid of fire and chip it into the shape of a tomahawk, and then grind it down to very thin blades. According to the thinness of the stone and the size of it, so is its value. It takes years of work to grind a very good tomahawk stone, and such stones are treasured throughout the east of New Guinea. Traders bring to Woodlark Island to barter for tomahawk stones the shells which are very general currency throughout the island and which are worn as armlets. There are two kinds of shell currency, small white shells with black spots, and red shells which are found on the underside of a projecting ledge of coral reef. These latter have to be got by diving.

Gold had just been discovered at Woodlark Island, and one evening the natives who were collecting insects for me brought in some gold found at the junction of two creeks. Collecting was not proving very profitable at the time and for a while I turned to digging, taking up a claim which I worked for about six months, getting about £250 in gold. I decided then (1896) to come Home on a visit. My friend Mr. Barnard in Queensland had given up collecting and I bought his collection from him, paying him, I think, £500 for it.

Coming to England for the second time I again found myself with no intention at all of settling down in the ways of civilisation. I stayed but three months in London, during which time I signed an agreement with the Hon. Walter Rothschild, who was very much pleased with the collecting work I had already done, to undertake definite investigations on his behalf in certain districts. On returning to Australia I brought a younger brother, Mr. W. G. Meek, out with me to assist in collecting.

CANOE, TROBRIANDS.

CEREMONIAL HOUSE, MILNE BAY.

CHAPTER V

LEARNING TO NAVIGATE; AND SOME COLLECTING IN THE LOUISIADE GROUP

UPON my return to Australia, with very definite collecting plans in view, I found that the carrying out of those plans was destined to be a good deal interrupted whilst I learned to navigate. Navigation I did not attempt to learn, as I might have done easily, from some one with knowledge of the art and of the South Seas: but blundered into the school of experience. I suppose that throughout I have always taken up the attitude of under-estimating difficulties and dangers. Really it is that I do not see them until they come so close to hand that they must be seen. Possibly this has helped rather than hindered in dealing with the natives. Trouble with them usually arises from " nerves " on the part of the white man. He expects that the natives will prove savage, bloodthirsty, treacherous, and unconsciously acts in just such a way as to bring out those traits in them. If he had confidence in the natives, or simply did not think about their character, one way or the other, probably there would be much less trouble. But in going out to encounter the sea it is well to be armed with knowledge.

I had resolved to become independent as far as possible of the little trading schooners of the islands on my third collecting trip. So towards the end of 1896 at Sydney I bought a twenty-feet whaleboat and brought it with me by the steamer to Cairns, where I outfitted for the new expedition. At Cairns I engaged as helpers three Kanakas, Tom, Joe, and Luke, and a black boy named Jimmy. Then we all took steamer to Samarai and there took in stores, and in 1897 set out in the whaleboat for Woodlark Island.

I had no knowledge at all of navigation and had not even a compass aboard. My idea of the best way of getting to Woodlark Island was to follow the shoreline of New Guinea around by way of the Trobriand Islands and work round from there to Woodlark Island. Thus, I reasoned out, I would never be out of sight of land. From Samarai to Woodlark was quite an easy run for any one who understood navigation, but because I did not wish to lose sight of land I conceived the idea of going by way of the Trobriands.

I was to learn in the school of experience that navigation was not a matter that could be taken in that casual way. As far as the Trobriands we got along all right with favourable winds, but from the Trobriands to Woodlark Island we encountered a dead-ahead wind, and had to face the certainty that, since it was the trade wind usual to the season, it would neither moderate in strength nor change in direction for some months. The whaleboat was very

LEARNING TO NAVIGATE

low in the water, as it was loaded down with a lot of gear. I decided to divide the burden and chartered a small cutter to carry the gear. Then taking the four boys with us in the whaleboat we (my brother and I) set sail from the Trobriands. Promptly we were driven back to our starting point. That was the history of several succeeding days—an attempt to make some progress, succeeding perhaps until the afternoon, and then being driven back to where we came from. Finally one day I lost sight of the cutter, and, night falling, I found I was unable to reach the point that I had started from, and I steered by the moon to another island called Keetava. I reached the shore in safety, but was in rather a sad plight with no food and no matches to build a fire, as all our stores were in the cutter, the *Charm*. The natives, however, came down to the beach and gave us turtle eggs and yams, and lent us a fire-stick, so that we were fairly comfortable. The next morning the *Charm* turned up, the crew being pleasantly surprised to find me alive, as they thought that I had been lost during the night. The next day we managed to get to Fergusson Island and from there to Goodenough Island, but I was not able to get to Woodlark Island. Making the best of things at Goodenough Island, I formed a camp and started collecting in December 1896.

There is a mountain there which I climbed to a great height looking for a particular species of Bird of Paradise. I took with me as bearers some of the coast people and one of my Kanaka boys. The other boys I left on the coast collecting. On the way up the mountain, going through the garden of a village, I encountered a native who threatened me with a stone axe and tried to turn me back. I kept going steadily forward though he brandished the axe in my face. He came so close that I feared at one time that I should have to shoot him, but when he saw that I was not to be either scared or turned back he became more friendly and invited me to go with him up to the village. There I sat with my back to a house, so as to prevent a surprise attack from the rear, and palavered with the natives. I made them bring me some coco-nuts and induced them to be fairly friendly. They had never seen a white man before. I was anxious to see if a particular Bird of Paradise, called *Paradisea decora*, occurred there, but I did not discover it, so I came back to my camp. I found my Kanakas all in great dread of the natives, who had been threatening them with their tomahawks.

At this camp I had a big stock of "trade," that is to say, tobacco, knives and tomahawks. My riches were a great temptation to the natives to loot the camp. One morning the chief of the coast village and his son came in to warn me that the inhabitants of a Bush village were coming to attack us. He got up a tree to keep watch, and we also kept a sharp look-out upon the scrub which was all round our camp,

LEARNING TO NAVIGATE

which was in an open grass clearing. The attack did not come off, but it was quite clear from the marks that we found in the scrub afterwards that the inhabitants in the Bush above had collected for an attack, and had probably postponed it when they saw that we were ready and would not be taken by surprise.

I stayed six weeks at Goodenough Island, doing a certain amount of collecting. But the natives were never really friendly, and finally, hearing that I was in danger, a Government patrol boat came out and took all of us back to Samarai. It was the only occasion on which I had to be "rescued," and even then the need of rescue was not very apparent to me. From Samarai I sent my collection of birds and insects away and caught a trading schooner to Woodlark Island, taking my whaleboat aboard the vessel. I made one steady resolve on this voyage, and that was not to be such a fool again as to attempt a sea voyage without any knowledge of navigation.

At this time, because I suppose of the long-continued hostility of the natives and the poor state of my health, I was inclined to take rather a gloomy view of the climate and its perils. My "health" notes in December 1896 recorded—

"The blood in this country seems to go wrong very quickly. If things continue at the same rate as these last two days I shall be unable to walk in a few days, on account of big sores and swollen ankles. I can press my thumb into the ankle and leave an impression more than half an inch deep. We have been free from fever, comparatively. So far I have not had a touch of it, but perhaps to make up for it I had the swollen feet. By way of remedy at first I tried iodoform pure, then pure carbolic with vaseline, then zinc ointment. Then, on Christmas Day, I accidentally discovered something that may perhaps be of use to any one who finds himself in the same position as I was. For three nights I had had scarcely any sleep at all, on account of the pain in my feet and ankles, brought on by the sores. On Christmas morning I was completely worn out and felt quite unable to work. My feet would ache like a dull toothache for a few minutes, then something would start a pain like red-hot needles being run into them. By way of experiment I mixed some carbolic with salad oil (about four of oil to one of acid) and put it on. It seemed to take the pain away within a few minutes, and after that I had a sound sleep and felt another man altogether."

In addition to the uneasiness caused by illness in my own camp there were disheartening reports from others. When I had come across to Samarai from Cooktown the previous November, a party of five diggers from Townsville arrived at the same time in a half-decked cutter, and proceeded up the N.E. coast, intending to try and get up the Moosa River. I heard at this time that one was dead and two half dead; so ill they had to be carried off the boat

LEARNING TO NAVIGATE

on coming ashore. It took them five weeks getting up the river thirty-five miles.

However, these troubles notwithstanding, I kept on with my work, my chief anxiety being that the rush of diggers to the South Sea Islands consequent upon the discoveries of gold would bring so much population that there would be an end of any chance of collecting in virgin territory.

At this time I began to take Natural History notes with some degree of method, communicating them by letters to the Tring Museum from my various camps : usually I sent to Dr. Jordan my notes on the habits of insects, to Dr. Hartert my notes on the habits of birds.

The most interesting notes I made at Goodenough Island were : that the natives were very lazy as collectors, differing in that from the people of the Trobriands and of Fergusson Island, who had been very keen on sending us in specimens. The *Paradisea decora* does not occur there. I believe it only occurs at Nadi (Mt. Edgwaba), and Mt. Kilherran on the north of Fergusson Island. The Goodenough Island natives call it by another name and only know it by seeing other natives wearing its plumage in their armlets.

I found at Goodenough Island nine good specimens of the very rare *Pitta finchi*, and eight of a new species of Frogmouth, described by Dr. Hartert as *Podargus intermedius*. The male differs slightly from the female. There is found there a dove, new to me, reddish chocolate in colour and barred from bill to tip of tail.[1] Among the lepidoptera there was one very fine large Zygaenid, with white wings and black border and black veins with large blue spot at the base of both wings. It is an extremely handsome insect and only occurs in one place so far as my boys could find. The boys were very stupid the first three weeks or so, but afterwards they were capital lepidoptera collectors, and I think would have found this Zygaenid elsewhere if it had existed.[2]

I arrived at Woodlark Island early in 1897 and camped at a place called Burgees, in March 1897, close to where the chief gold mines are now. This was not a very good spot for collecting, but I had to stay there as I could not get the natives to take me on to Salova. My whaleboat had very little freeboard and would not carry all my gear. It was impossible for a long time to obtain native canoes for the carriage of the gear. The delay in getting these canoes kept me at Burgees longer than I wished. I occupied the time usefully if not profitably in studying

[1] This is the female of the very rare *Macropygia nigrirostris*.—E. H.

[2] The Zygaenid is *Hemiscia meeki*, Rothschild, *Nov. Zool.*, 1896, p. 326. The male is much smaller than the female, the white areas of the wings being replaced by short buff bands. Mr. Meek also discovered on Fergusson a fine Geometer, *Milionia elegans*, R. & J., *Nov. Zool.*, 1895, with blue-black wings, the forewing being banded with white and the hindwing bearing a red patch at the abdominal margin.—K. J.

the natives. Occasionally I pleased them by catching fish for them with dynamite plug. The natives there have a system of fishing with a poison root. The root of this plant is crushed until it yields a milky juice. If this juice is put freely in a pool of water it seems to have a narcotic effect on the fish, for they come stupefied to the surface.

My method of fishing was that which is universally followed by the white man in the South Seas when he wishes to obtain fish for food, that is to explode dynamite under the water. The number of one-armed white men in the South Sea Islands will strike one as extraordinary until one understands that the loss of an arm is one of the penalties of carelessness in the use of dynamite for fishing.

It was whilst I was moving from Burgees to Fergusson Island that I saw the end of my whaleboat, the possession of which, up to then, had given me much more adventure than profit. We were sailing along the coast outside the reef when, at a spot which I afterwards learnt was dangerous, a great breaker washed us clean out of the boat, that is to say, myself, a New Guinea boy, and a Kanaka. An Australian aboriginal was left alone in the boat, which was waterlogged and drifted away from us. The New Guinea boy was a smart enough sailor to seize hold of a couple of oars and he came swimming to my help and we got to the boat. We had just succeeded in doing this when she overturned again.

We hung on to the keel all the morning until she drifted inshore. The shore there consisted of great cliffs of coral which had been hollowed out underneath the sea level by the action of the waves. It left little chance of landing with the heavy surf that was then beating. Fortunately I spied a bit of a shelving beach, and on the crest of a big wave made for that. The wave curled over me and sent me shooting down towards the bottom. I thought of the razor-sharp edges of the steep coral cliffs, of the great hollowed-out caves beneath the water-line where I would be battered to death without a chance of escape, and concluded that I had collected my last butterfly. I kept my breath stubbornly, however, though my chest and head were nigh to bursting, and after what seemed a million years I came to the surface. But in a second the surf seized me again and I was sucked down to a coral ledge which bit cruelly into my leg. Perhaps the new sharp pain of this saved me. I kicked out vigorously and got to the surface once again. This time the waves were kind and flung me on to the little shelving beach.

I got to shore with very little breath, but with a deep sense of thankfulness. The boys were all saved except the Australian boy, who perished. The natives who had watched our struggles without attempting to help us gave us something to eat, and we managed to make ourselves fairly comfortable, but I will carry to my grave marks of the wounds that I received in the battering that the surf gave me on that coral reef. The whaleboat was smashed to splinters.

We made a camp there, and my young brother, who had travelled overland, joined me at the camp, together with another man whom I had engaged from Cooktown. The collecting, however, was poor. Being deprived of the whaleboat I arranged now to purchase a small cutter, of some nine tons, called the *Calliope*, and with her I went back to my old Nadi camp, where I got some specimens of Birds of Paradise. I stayed there for some six weeks and then went to Samarai, from whence I sent on my collections to the Tring Museum.

In Woodlark Island I found several birds that were new to me. Among them was a lory, called *Lorius hypoenochrous*, a fine falcon of the group of the Peregrine-Falcons (*Falco ernesti*), and others.

On Fergusson Island not less than sixty-three species of birds were found, some of which were very rare, and a few quite unknown.[1]

The black and white flycatcher (*Monarcha chalybeocephala*), of which I found two only on Woodlark

[1] On Fergusson, besides the beautiful *Paradisea decora*, two kinds of Manucodia, *i. e. Manucodia comrii* and *Phonygammus hunsteini*, were found. One of the rarest birds is an Ant-Thrush, *Pitta finschi*, and the *Myzomela forbesi*, the male of which is black, with the underside of the wings white, while the young ones are brown with red cap and throat. A Honey-eater (*Melilestes fergussonis*), the Frogmouth (*Podargus intermedius*), a fine little Parrakeet (*Cyclopsittacus virago*), and a Pigeon (*Ptilopus lewisi vicinus*) were new.—E. H.

Island, occurs on Fergusson Island also. The female has a brick-red breast and throat. I caught two species of brown *Pachycephala*, i.e. *P. dubia* and *P. fortis*. I captured one good specimen of the hawk of which I had previously shot a bad specimen (*Baza reinwardti*), also some *Paradisea decora*, but mostly young males or females.

My next voyage was to St. Aignan in the Louisiades in August 1897. We camped there in Bogoya Harbour, where I got some new birds and a fine new *Ornithoptera—Troides coelestis* Mr. Rothschild called it. It is a magnificent butterfly, very large in size, blue and black in colour. I was very jubilant at this discovery, for it was my first new *Ornithoptera*. The species is still very rare. It was obtained in very mountainous country, though my camp at the time was near the coast.

I bred here two specimens of a beautiful large *Charagia* similar to the one from the Trobriands.[1] Among the smaller species of lepidoptera I found many things new to me, and a rather handsome *Delias* which only occurs on the tops of the hills. Of this I obtained a long series, but unfortunately only one female. Among the birds new to me there were a large cuckoo, three species of flycatcher, one *Pachycephala*, and one pigeon.

The first specimens of the above-mentioned *Orni-*

[1] The St. Aignan form is *Charagia marginatus misimanus*, Roths., *Nov. Zool.*, 1898, p. 219.—K. J.

LEARNING TO NAVIGATE

thoptera were obtained on August 29th, 1897. The insect resembles *urvilliana* in colour, being perhaps a shade lighter and brighter, and seemed to me to have much narrower belts of blue on the forewing, while it was not so large as the specimens found in New Ireland and the Solomons. It was remarkable that the Woodlark Island specimens were green, while those of St. Aignan were blue, though the latter were much further away from the home of *urvilliana* (New Ireland and the Solomons). The underside of the hindwing of the St. Aignan specimens had a most decided greenish appearance, yet the insect was most certainly distinct from other New Guinea specimens. This difference in colour was very striking, for I had been accustomed to the green insect,[1] which I had taken or seen from Cape Vogel on the mainland to the Engineer Group (the nearest group of islands west of St. Aignan's excepting the Conflicts). At

---

[1] New Guinea and the islands close to it are inhabited by *Papilio priamus poseidon*, which has a green male. Australia, the Southern Moluccas, Key and Aru Islands, and New Britain are also inhabited by forms of *priamus* with green males. On New Ireland, New Hanover and all the Solomon Islands the males are blue, this being *P. priamus urvillianus*. On the Northern Moluccas the males are orange, on the island of Obi greenish blue, and likewise greenish blue on Duke of York, in between New Britain and New Ireland. The form from St. Aignan, with its blue male, agrees best with Australian specimens, apart from the difference in colour. We now regard all these differently coloured forms as geographical varieties of one species. The name of *Ornithoptera* unfortunately cannot be employed in science, as there are two older names available for these insects: *Papilio* and *Troides*.—K. J.

the Engineer Group, where I captured a number, the females run nearly black, having generally black forewings, while the females of the insect at St. Aignan resembled the females of *urvilliana* so much that I could detect no difference, except perhaps the former were slightly smaller. I also obtained larvæ and pupæ. They resembled the larvæ of the Queensland insect, having semi-transparent red spikes. The larvæ of the Fergusson Island insect differed from the St. Aignan insects in having no bright colours.

My observations inclined me to the opinion that there are two species of blue *Ornithoptera*, but I couldn't be certain until I had more specimens to examine; I had about fourteen females and three males. I found out that the females were of two distinct sizes and of the males, two are equally large, while the third is much smaller and a trifle darker. The sizes resemble a large *richmondia* and an ordinary *cassandira*. The smaller males are slightly darker in colour, and one has two small yellow marks near the outside of the hindwings.[1]

The Cuscus on St. Aignan rather reversed the order of things in having a brown male and dark steel-grey female.[2]

---

[1] These differences are merely individual.—K. J.

[2] Mr. Meek collected sixty-five species of birds on St. Aignan, among them a new Flycatcher (*Gerygone rosseliana onerosa*), a new White-eye (*Zosterops aignani*), a new form of long-tailed dove (*Macropygia doreya cunctata*), and other rare species only found in the Louisiade group of islands.—E. H.

LEARNING TO NAVIGATE

One of my collectors brought in an *Agarista*, similar to the one with an orange spot in the hind-wings from Fergusson and Goodenough Islands. This insect seemed a trifle different, the orange patch on the underwings being slightly more conspicuous, and to me the spot appeared to vary somewhat in shape.[1]

The common *Nyctalemon* (black, bronze and bluey-white) occurred on St. Aignan, though so far from the mainland. It took after the Queensland insect in being very "coppery" in colour.

I stayed at St. Aignan some three months, and then took the cutter *Calliope* to Rossel Island at the extreme end of the Louisiades group. This place had rather a bad reputation in the South Seas because of the wreck there once of a ship with a Chinese crew. The natives kept the Chinese as prisoners on the wreck and ate them one by one, quite after the manner of the Cyclops with the followers of Odysseus.

My New Guinea boys were very much perturbed at the thought of going to Rossel Island, because it bore such an evil reputation. The Government ketch *Murua* was at the time anchored at St. Aignan, on its way thither to quieten some tribes who had been desolating other villages, killing man, woman,

---

[1] *Immetalia saturata meeki*, Roths., *Nov. Zool.*, 1896, p. 32, described from Fergusson. The specimens from St. Aignan do not differ from those obtained on Fergusson and Goodenough.—K. J.

child, pig, dog, and fowl. However, I did not anticipate trouble with the natives, after the Government boat had been there.

But the reputation of the place was so bad that I did not think it wise to trust the natives too much; and the natives themselves did not trust one another, for it was quite usual for the young fellows of a village who felt that they were in particularly good eating condition to refuse to sleep in the village, and to take to canoes at evening-tide and sleep out somewhere on the reef where they would be more safe.

Rossel Island is very mountainous and the natives are in many respects different from those of the mainland of New Guinea. They are an agricultural people mainly. In the villages the two sexes are separated into different quarters. The morals of the people are good usually, but there is a custom there which I do not remember having observed anywhere else in the South Seas, that of setting aside a certain number of women who are accessible to all the males of the community. This imitation of the Japanese yoshiwarra I have not found elsewhere in the South Seas, though it is not unusual in some of the islands for strangers, especially white men, to be offered women as concubines. Apart from the public women, the females of Rossel Island seem very shy and are difficult to see, it seeming to be the custom to keep them from the view of strangers.

The Rossel Island natives put up a house for us

and we camped close to the beach, keeping always a careful watch lest the village butcher should make a sudden call on us. There were in camp my brother, myself and a Mr. Eichhorn, and four New Guinea boys. We did not collect very much at this place in the way of insects, but I discovered several new birds, including a new *Pitta* and a rare kingfisher.[1]

We suffered from fever very badly at intervals. Perhaps the diet may have had something to do with that. We lived always on tinned meat, rice and flour, with vegetables when we could get them. Alcohol was not used in the camp except for medicine.

I did not get very much of new Natural History observation at Rossel Island. But there were many things there which I had not seen off the mainland, such as the racket-tailed kingfisher (blue and white). While I was away getting yams and boys for Rossel Island, I left my men on a small island S.E. of St. Aignan, named Kimita. They managed to get there three more males of the blue *Ornithoptera*. The natives of Rossel Island were very positive about the *Ornithoptera* being on their island upon my showing them a specimen, but I put no faith in what they said, for to them a small bird is a small bird, and to perhaps a dozen species they give the same name—the same,

---

[1] The *Pitta* was described by Mr. Rothschild as *Pitta meeki*, and Mr. Meek discovered also the nest and eggs of this bird, which were described in *Nov. Zool.*, 1899, p. 80. The kingfisher one might say, the most beautiful of the racket-tailed species, is the rare *Tanysiptera rosseliana*.—E. H.

of course, with butterflies. However, they were right for once.

I expected to get great assistance from the natives, but they brought in only a few lizards and a Cuscus. Among the birds I got the most notable were two species of brown and grey *Pachycephala*;[1] the *Pitta meeki* is something similar to the Fergusson Island bird, but slightly smaller, with rufous cap and nape and with greenish brown back, belly bright red as other species. We took only one *Ornithoptera*, a male (similar to the St. Aignan one), and I saw one female only. One can imagine how scarce they were when with five men collecting we only captured one specimen and saw one other.

After some two months at Rossel Island I made my way to Sudest, where there was at the time a great fleet of pearl-divers, the divers being white men and Manilla men, that being before the coming of the Japanese diver. In those days the life of the pearl-sheller was easy. The natives had no idea of the value of pearls. They could not be pierced, as shells were, with the native drills: and Nature had not left holes in them, so they could not be strung on to an armlet. When the first white trader appeared he is credited

[1] They were both described as new by myself and called *P. rosseliana* and *P. meeki*. The *Endoliisoma* was also a new species, and described by me as *E. rostratum*, and there were also a new fan-tailed Flycatcher (*Rhipidura louisiadensis*), another new small Flycatcher (*Gerygone rosseliana*), a new *Myzomela* (*M. albigula*), and a new form of Parrot (*Geoffroyas aruensis cyanicarpus*).—E. H.

LEARNING TO NAVIGATE

with having filled a pickle-jar with pearls at a cost of two or three pounds of tobacco, and the natives thought the white man a fool for buying such rubbish.

I went over to the pearl-divers' camp with the main purpose of replenishing my stores, but stayed there awhile for the sake of the company. The white divers were very convivial and, after long intervals of living among savages, white company was very grateful.

The natives of Sudest are now very civilised. In the early days there were gold-fields there, and after the white man had exhausted the best ore the natives took on the work and proved very clever at it, especially at fossicking in old workings. The natives of Sudest are not cannibals, but used to be eaten very extensively, having been generally the victims of more warlike tribes of the New Guinea mainland.

At Sudest I discovered some new birds, in particular a new Podargus, a new parrot, and a new night-jar.[1] But I found no new *Ornithoptera*. After staying there some three months I went back to Samarai and was very nearly lost at sea. It was at the time of the change of monsoon, and the change came in with a great storm of wind and rain and lightning. The

---

[1] The new birds from Sudest were the following: *Chibia carbonaria dejecta*, Hart.; *Pachycephala alberti*, Hart.; *Graucalus hypoleucus louisiadensis*, Hart.; *Endoliisoma amboinense tagulanum*, Hart.; *Rhipidura setosa nigromentalis*, Hart.; *Myiagra nupta, Myzomela nigrita louisiadensis* and *Zosterops meeki*, Hart.—E. H.

lightning in particular was most alarming. It played around the boat as a cat plays with her paws around a mouse. Stroke after stroke seemed to just miss our little craft as it staggered and sobbed through the sea. At times I could smell the sulphur (or rather ozone) of the lightning flashes. But it all ended with the morning and we got safely to Samarai.

I was fortunate, by the way, to have finished on Rossel Island at the time I did, as just after I had left news came through that of three boat-loads of boys (about one hundred) taken from Rossel Island to Mombare, all had died but about ten. Men and boys were dying there then at a dreadful rate from dysentery. If I had been on the spot at Rossel Island at the time when the news came through, possibly the natives would have made a victim of me as a measure of part requital. That is their way. If they blame the white man for any evil that has befallen them they are anxious to wreak vengeance on any white man who is handy. To a very inconvenient extent their ideas make each white man his brother's keeper.

From Samarai I went back to Cooktown for a long spell. By this time I had become fairly well used to the ways of exploration in the South Sea Islands. I could navigate a little, at any rate I knew enough not to venture out to sea without compass and charts. I was beginning to understand the ways of the natives, and I was beginning to feel my feet financially. At Cooktown I was married, and my wife and I stayed there for our honeymoon. My young brother, who had suffered very much from fever, decided that he would return to London, but I had not the smallest desire to get back to the conventional life of civilisation. So far I had been learning to collect rather than actually collecting. I formed plans for some great inland expeditions, feeling that I had now learned through past mistakes how to win greater successes in the future.

CHAPTER VI

A VISIT TO THE SOLOMON ISLANDS

It was in 1898 that I turned my back on civilisation again, determined that this time I should explore some territory new to the naturalist, and that I should not be delayed or thwarted by any experiments in navigation, an art of which I had now mastered the rudiments.

I went round to the site of my old camp at Nadi for the purpose of recruiting boys as collectors. I had a warm welcome from the natives there, who remembered me perfectly. Having got a good gang of boys to help in the work of collecting, I made an expedition to Milne Bay, where I designed a camp of a somewhat more permanent type than any to which I had been as yet accustomed. We built not only a native house, but also laid out a garden, planting in addition to the native taro and yams, some beans and melons.

The boys whom I had brought with me I used to send out collecting both birds and insects. It was here that I made my second discovery of a new *Ornithoptera*, the tailed *Troides meridionalis*. It is a very beautiful butterfly, green and black and gold in colour, and is still very rare. Another most interesting discovery here was a rare *Papilio*, called the *Papilio laglaizei*. This was not new, but had not been encountered before in that district. It is a butterfly that mimics the moth in some respects, and is black and bronze in colour. A discovery that was named after me was the *Orgyris meeki*. I got a male specimen of this large blue insect at Milne Bay on this occasion (1898). I did not get a female specimen until the year 1910.

The natives were very friendly at Milne Bay, and I stayed there some five months. I had some advantage of my garden, which yielded fine crops of melons, which I used to bring to Samarai for my friends. I recall here encountering the tail-end of the famous hurricane of 1898. Hurricanes, however, are not particularly common in the South Seas. Usually there we have the benefit of fairly regular trade winds. There are two different seasons, that of the South-East monsoon, usually accompanied by fine weather, and lasting from April to December, and that of the North-West monsoon, during which storms may be expected. The North-West monsoon season continues during January, February, and March.

This hurricane of 1898 was so severe that sea-birds were cast up dead on the beach, and trees uprooted in all directions. I had good reason to remember it, for after two days of raging wind which appeared to come from all points of the compass, there was a lull which seemed to mark the end of the storm. The glass was still very low, but I paid no attention to its warning and put out for Samarai. We were barely out when the wind came down, as solid as a wall, from the South-West, and the boat went almost on her beam ends. I tried to lower the mainsail, but the throat halyards jammed, and it seemed as though we were doomed. But my New Guinea boy, good sailor that he was, shinned up the mast and let slip the sheet and we were safe.

My notes at Milne Bay this year (1899) were mostly regarding the habits of butterflies. I had taken one perfect male of *Ornithoptera meridionalis*, also one male specimen of the large blue butterfly (*Orgyris meeki*) which pupates under the ground at the trunk of the food-plant (the tree on which the mistletoe lives). It is much larger than any Queensland species, and has a much longer tail. The collection of lepidoptera far excelled the Fergusson Island collections. There was one species of Cyrestis, collected on very high ground, with a comparatively long tail. The underside had black stripes running to a point similar to some species of *Papilio*, and the underside or hindwing was black with greenish-copper markings. Then I got two specimens of a small green *Antherea*, about two-and-a-half inches across, and another new (to me) species of chocolate *Charagia*. In all, the collection of lepidoptera amounted to about 20,000 specimens of such things

HOUSE, MILNE BAY.

as the handsome *Tenaris* with black hind-wings and large blue eyes, also of the chestnut-brown *Tenaris*, rather large with yellow patch across the end of the fore-wing and two large eyes on the underside of the hind-wing.

From Milne Bay I made a trip up the North-East coast, where I found the natives were very wild. My purpose was to buy curios and to collect specimens of Birds of Paradise. The natives there at that time had little or no iron, and were very keen on getting anything either of iron or steel. With a small piece of iron one could get very great quantities of native shell-money, and rare curios which it is now almost impossible to secure. The collections were fairly satisfactory.

Most previous collectors had used New Guinea boys, who only shoot what they see, and do not bother to ascertain the note of the bird. A New Hebrides boy I had shooting on this trip, got very many good things. He learned the notes of various birds; then, when he came to a clearing, where he could shoot without being too close, he would sit down and call up the birds with their own note. He was especially successful with ground-birds.

I found that there were in this district two species of Eupetes, one much larger than the other. The smaller is blue-slate with white throat. The other occurs at a much higher altitude, is much larger, and differs from other species in having chestnut colour on the neck and part of the back.[1] There was also found here a mountain ground-thrush. The sexes differ very much, but it was not unlike the ground-thrush that occurs in the mountains in Queensland, of which I had got a specimen from Chester River, Cape York.[2]

On this trip I shot a huge Crowned Pigeon (*goura*) whilst on the nest with the rifle, and got one egg (they do not lay more). In appearance the egg of the goura pigeon is similar to a very small crocodile's egg, being hard and very glossy in appearance. I shot a great number of the birds afterwards for eating purposes, but, of course, did not shoot another brooding mother.

At this time I decided to " settle down " definitely in the South Seas, and to combine collecting with farming. I bought a farm close to Samarai with an area of about 160 acres. Subsequently I purchased the adjoining block of 140 acres. The land was covered with coco-nut palms and with good grass. It was my idea to run a dairy-farm for the purpose of supplying Samarai with milk and butter. Cattle do well in New Guinea, especially in coco-nut palm country. From Sydney I obtained a herd of about 100 cattle, and I recruited a number of native boys to cut down the scrub, and thus improve the land. It seems to me that in New Guinea there is a great future for cattle-ranching. In the wild state of the

---

[1] *Êupetes castanonotus* and *E. caerulescens nigricrissus.*—E. H.
[2] *Cinclosoma ajax.*—E. H.

forest a very high cane-grass grows under the trees. After that has been burnt off or eaten off by cattle there comes a finer grass, and after that couch grass, which is excellent for cattle. It is quite easy in New Guinea to run a beast to the acre.

On my farm, in addition to the yield from dairy-farming and the copra from the coco-nuts, we obtained sweet potatoes and maize for the Samarai market. The main reason guiding me in taking to farm-life for a while, was that the Hon. Walter Rothschild had told me that he would not wish me to undertake any more collecting work for a couple of years, as he had so many collections in hand.

The farm venture was not very prosperous at first. I lost a great number of cattle coming up from Sydney in a storm, and afterwards pleuro broke out in my herd. But it did not need these minor misfortunes to convince me that I was not cut out for a farmer. The call of the adventurous life came again, and I was soon designing another collecting trip, again making a satisfactory arrangement with Mr. Rothschild.

In 1901 I made my first expedition to the Solomon Islands. The Solomon Islander was at the time somewhat more civilised than the Papuan. He was fairly prosperous as a trader in copra and in turtle-shell. There are two distinct types of native in the Solomons. At the west end of the Solomons, that is to say, at Bougainville and New Georgia, they are much darker than the Papuan. At the east end of the group they are more like the Papuan in colour and in character.

My first camp in the Solomons was at a village of Guadalcanar Island, where for the first time I tried the experiment of camping in the midst of the native houses. The old chief of the village obliged me by putting taboo marks on the doors of the huts of my party, thus protecting us from interference on the part of the resident natives. At Guadalcanar I stayed some six or seven weeks, making a fair collection. There I encountered for the first time a very handsome snake, called the king snake. It has a black head, and the neck is surrounded by a white band. Then follows a gold band. These bands of black, white, and gold, alternate on the body of the reptile. The king snake is very rare, and according to the stories of the natives is only seen when a chief has died. I got several specimens, which I sent to Europe.

In the Solomons the village residential houses are not so good as those of the Papuans, but their canoe houses are very much better. They have not much idea of sailing canoes, and very little idea of seacraft, but their very large war and trading canoes, which they drive by paddles, hold some forty of fifty men.

The Solomon Islanders, who are very warlike, have a bad reputation as cannibals and head-hunters.

A VISIT TO THE SOLOMON ISLANDS

Sorcery is rife in the villages, the magician or pouri-pouri man holding a sway of dread over men and women. It is a usual thing at the fall of night in a Solomon village, for the " medicine men " to take large branches of trees and beat the streets with them in order to frighten away evil spirits.

My collecting party at Guadalcanar consisted, besides myself, of Eichhorn, seven New Guinea boys and four New Hebrides boys. With a little training the New Guinea boy, or the Kanaka, makes a very good collector. I supply him with a black japanned collecting-box, a quantity of pins, a butterfly-net, and a number of pill-boxes for the smaller insects. These smaller insects he puts into the pill-boxes alive without touching them. The larger butterflies he kills and fixes into the collecting-box (which has a cork lining) with pins. My usual method would be to send the native collectors out at 7.30 in the morning, and they would stop out all day, returning after sundown, and handing over their collections to me then. I would examine what they had brought, killing all the little insects with cyanide and killing the big ones by injecting oxalic acid into their bodies. Then I would put them away until the next morning, and devote the day hours to their setting and packing.

Now that I had got into the ways of collecting, I very rarely attempted any work with the net myself, trusting to the boys to bring in what they might encounter, and sometimes instructing them as to some special specimen that they were likely to meet, and that I was anxious to obtain. At a later stage in collecting, I used to have acetylene lamps for the purpose of attracting moths by night. These would only be of value in mountainous districts. The insects collected would be packed up with naphthaline to dispatch to Europe.

My Natural History notes at Guadalcanar (1901) were not very notable. I captured a female *urvilliana* with *black*, not brown, fore-wings, showing distinct traces of the blue male. It is a thing I had been looking for for many years, and this was the nearest approach to both sexes in the one insect that I had ever seen.

From Guadalcanar I went to Ysabel Island, where I discovered a number of new birds, including a new large owl of a chestnut colour. The natives had told me about this bird, and that it was its custom to feed on the opossums in the Bush. I entrusted one native boy with a gun and some cartridges, asking him to obtain me a specimen, and promising him as a reward, if he did, ten arm-rings, which would be worth some two shillings each. He was successful in obtaining one, I think on the very last night before I left the island. It was quite a new species, the nearest to it before discovered being a bird found only in the Philippine Islands. In addition to this owl I discovered some seven or eight new birds, including a new *Podargus*, a new kingfisher and a new *Pitta*.[1]

In regard to insects I was also fairly fortunate, discovering one very fine *Papilio*, a female, which was named after me. A male specimen has not been discovered yet, and it will be one of my tasks in the future to search for one. No second specimen of the female has yet been found. It is a dark black butterfly with green spots. I obtained here also a number of the *Ornithoptera victoriae*, a very big butterfly which is still very rare. I have seen one specimen sold for twenty-two guineas. The boys got several specimens of this on the "blossom-trees," a kind of teak growing in that locality. By collecting in the mountains we got more males than females. The males, as soon as they hatch out, make for the mountains.

In addition to collecting, I did a little trading in turtle-shell and native shell-money, which proved fairly profitable. Altogether I was very pleased with my first venture in the Solomons. In the district which I had covered, nobody had previously collected birds, and there had been no systematic collection of butterflies, so it was practically virgin soil.

[1] The new owl is *Pseudoptynx solomonensis*, the *Podargus* is called *P. inexpectatus*, Hart., and the *Pitta* is the very remarkable *P. anerythra*, Rothsch. Besides these new birds, such rarities as *Nasiterna nanina* (a tiny little parrot), and *Zosterops metcalfei* were found. The birds of Ysabel are discussed and partly figured in *Nov. Zool.* 1902.—E. H.

The natural beauty of the Solomon group is very great. I can never forget the great Marabo Lagoon, a wide sheet of still clear water of dazzling blue, studded with thousands of islands, some big enough to give space for a tiny village, some with hardly enough surface above the water to give foothold to a horse. On most of these islands coco-nut palms, ivory nut-trees, and banana-trees flourished. But occasionally one was bare of trees, and then its coral boulders would be studded with orchids, the most common variety being a large white blossom with a blue tongue. Flower-life is not, however, very plentiful in the South Sea Islands, though they are extraordinarily rich in food-producing plants. This is exactly opposite to the conditions ruling on the Australian continent, where there is a very rich variety of flower-life, and an almost complete absence of plants valuable for food—I mean, of course, indigenous plants. The most striking flowers of the South Sea Islands are the orchids that I have referred to, and the hibiscus bloom, a handsome bell-shaped flower, commonly scarlet in colour, but having varieties in different colourings. It is, I dare say, common enough in European hot-houses. In the South Seas (and also on the coast of Australia, where it has been introduced) the hibiscus grows to a thick scrub. The native women of Papua are accustomed to decorate themselves with garlands of hibiscus as a sign that they wish to be courted.

After leaving the Solomons I returned to my farm in New Guinea, which was now a very flourishing proposition, as the gold rushes had brought a large white population to Woodlark Island and to Samarai, and we were able to set up a butchering trade. This did not exactly gain for me such a fortune as was won by Tyson in Australia in the early days of the gold rushes there. He, when everybody was abandoning business to search for nuggets, was wise enough to turn his attention to supplying the diggers with meat; and in doing that he set the foundations of the greatest fortune which has ever been acquired in Australia. I made no Tyson " millions," but this new demand for killing cattle made my little ranch fairly prosperous. For quite a long spell now I gave up collecting. Then the desire for adventure fired my blood again, and I planned the most adventurous trip that I had as yet undertaken. I determined to explore the country in the interior of New Guinea underneath the Owen Stanley ranges. After recruiting boys, I embarked on the *Calliope*, and we were making our way towards Manna Manna when I was stopped by the Government steamer. The authorities had an idea that my little ship, the *Calliope*, was not exactly seaworthy, and further made some objection to the terms on which I had recruited my natives.

It seemed like the intervention of Fate. I gave up the expedition, turned my thoughts back to farming, sold the *Calliope* and decided that I should make an end of collecting.

To some extent this decision was due, I think, to annoyance on my part with the Government authorities, and to the feeling that expeditions were going to be made impossible for the future to private parties. That annoyance was natural. Under the conditions which ruled at first in the South Sea Islands, white traders and collectors had come to consider that they had the right to be a "law unto themselves." They knew the country and the natives. They had established themselves in advance of any police or Government protection, and had come to fairly good relations with the aboriginals. On the whole, I think, that these conditions had been come to without very much cruelty. Now settled authority interfered with all kinds of rules and regulations, some of which were resented as unnecessary or even harmful.

It has to be admitted that a certain amount of what may be called "grandmotherly legislation" is necessary in Government dealings with the Papuans. The natives are children, and have to be treated as such; and the white men must be compelled to give them something more than fair play, something of considerateness and patience. The extent of the grandmotherly tradition in the Government officials' treatment of the Papuans is amusingly illustrated in a recent report from the Mekes district, when an official gravely chronicles;

"*December* 17.—Went through the village again this morning and found that in three instances several married couples and their children were living indiscriminately in the same house, and that this had caused trouble and scandal. Ordered those who had no houses (they were really too lazy to build them) to set about building houses for themselves immediately. A young male native came to me and complained that a certain man in the village was keeping a young girl as a slave and would not allow her to marry. Inquired into the matter and discovered that what the boy said was quite correct. This man had an extensive garden and kept the girl simply as a drudge, and would not allow any one to approach her on the question of marriage. One suitor, more courageous than the others, went and spoke to the girl, and the guardian gave him a thrashing for his trouble. I called the girl up and found that she was a young woman of about 28 years of age. She informed me that she wished many times to get married, but her relative would not allow her to do so. I ordered the relative to place no further hindrance in the way of the young woman getting a husband, and announced to the village chiefs that the girl was now eligible for marriage, and if any young man desired her, and such feeling was reciprocated on the part of the young woman, that nothing was to occur to prevent the marriage. The poor girl was most grateful and happy at the announcement that freed her from serfdom. Have made a note of this to the Assistant Resident Magistrate so that he can keep the matter in mind and see if the girl is married on next visit."

In my case I was quite sure that the *Calliope* was seaworthy. I was at any rate confiding my own life to her, and I should not have done that if I had thought that she was unfitted for her work. My "boys," too, were quite satisfied with their conditions of employment. I had always got on very well with my collecting gangs in the past, and "boys" who had been with me once were willing to re-engage if the chance offered.

My annoyance was, I hold, natural. Yet I am willing to confess now that it was not justified. There had to be an end made of the old conditions in the South Seas. Authority had to come and, coming, it had to inflict some individual hardships. At the time I did not see this. I went back to farming at Samarai in a fit of the " sulks."

PORT MORESBY, PAPUA.

To face p. 116.

CHAPTER VII

INLAND NEW GUINEA—THE NATIVES AND MEASLES

AFTER being turned back from my projected trip to the mountains of British New Guinea by the resentment which I had felt at the Government official's criticism of my *Calliope*, and his objection to the terms of my recruiting agreement, I put in a year on the farm and by that time became thoroughly tired of a quiet, humdrum life. I planned, therefore, another expedition, buying the *Hekla*, a pearling boat, for £400, and recruiting a number of coast-boys and inland boys for a big expedition to the inland Stanley Ranges. At Port Moresby I purchased gear and stores and also engaged a Malay, partly to assist as a collector and partly to act as a guide, for he had some knowledge of the interior.

From Port Moresby we made our way along the coast to Manna Manna, where I laid the *Hekla* up and engaged canoes to take my gear up the river as far as possible. After the river ceased to be navigable I engaged over sixty carriers and we struck inland, making slow progress through rough country. As soon as we reached to the foot-hills which spread below the Stanley ranges, the difficulties of inland exploration began to develop in real earnest. At a village called Inawa the natives were in a state of great alarm at the advent of strangers. It seemed that they had suffered recently very much from the depredations of hostile tribes from the hills. They were so afraid of the hill men that I found it impossible to obtain carriers willing to march further inland. My coastal carriers also refused to go further. What with their fear and that of the Inawa men the position seemed desperate. The plan I had formed for penetrating to the interior was to retain, throughout the whole course of the expedition, the collecting boys and what I might call my " staff," and to trust to hiring local carriers to carry our gear and provisions stage by stage inland. It would have added much to the difficulties of organisation if I had attempted to bring the same gang of carriers right up from the coast, besides subjecting them to grave peril from the hill tribes.

When the system which I had worked out so carefully broke down, through the timidity of the tribes near the coast regarding the tribes further inland, I was for a time nonplussed, but I could not think of abandoning an expedition which had cost me so much trouble and expense. I decided to make an effort in another direction, and, obtaining the permission of the chief of Inawa, I went forward by myself, and from the tribes further inland I obtained carriers, whom I dispatched back to Inawa to carry up my stuff.

I have been told that it was a very risky thing to

INLAND NEW GUINEA

penetrate thus into disturbed and possibly hostile country without any escort. Perhaps, in theory, it was. All that I can say is that I encountered no very serious difficulties or dangers, and the success of the plan made all the difference between giving up a costly enterprise without result or carrying it through to a happy end.

This process of going forward after carriers had to be repeated again and again. At each stage I found that the people who were situated on the coast side did not dare to march forward inland, and it was necessary for me to leave my main camp, to strike inland by myself and send back for the outfit and for the native boys who were my collectors.

Eventually after some six weeks' hard and venturous work I got as far as Okuma, which is about sixty miles inland and is about 2000 feet high. The foot-hill country around was very rough. It seemed to be built on the "switchback" principle. One fold of hills was followed by another. You climbed with great difficulty a hill 1000 feet high only to have to descend again into a valley and face another struggling ascent. Days of laborious marching meant very little net gain, either in altitude or in distance from the coast.

At Okuma I thought that I was blocked for good, as the natives refused absolutely to help me further. Finally, after much persuasion, I induced the chief of the village to come on with me to a place called

Bwoidunna, a village some two days' march further inland. Here I was able to recruit carriers who went down towards the coast to Okuma and brought my baggage along. I was now some 3000 feet high, and I was encouraged by the sight of a very beautiful butterfly, *Papilio weiskei*, named after a German collector who had spent some months in the district previously. I was anxious to obtain specimens of it, and I determined to make my headquarters' camp at that spot with a secondary camp at a higher elevation.

My camp at Bwoidunna was on a much more ambitious scale than any that I had previously had in New Guinea; and I found my stay there very comfortable. The natives were friendly and extremely obliging. I recollect particularly one old native of that village who, for some reason or other, took a fancy to me and insisted on bringing me a present of some native product every day. (Sometimes a chicken, sometimes a yam, sometimes a butterfly.) The natives were so kind, indeed, that they would go without things themselves to keep us in comforts.

The climate on the hills of New Guinea is very fine. There is no fever. The nights are cool and the days warm and bright. There is undoubtedly a comfortable future for white people in New Guinea when they learn to utilise hill stations as is done in India.

The extra demands made on the food-supply of the

PAPUANS WITH TOBACCO PIPE.

To face p. 115.

village by my large camp soon made it necessary to forage for food elsewhere, and I kept a team of boys constantly at work penetrating to higher villages and bringing food from the mountains above. The most favoured currency there was coarse salt. On the coast one conducts most transactions with the natives on a currency of tobacco, but on the mountains the natives grow their own tobacco and seem to have always done so.[1] I found in the hill country of New Guinea, where they had never heard of the white man, and the white man had never before penetrated, that native tobacco was grown. They rarely subject it to any process of curing, except when they are making preparations for a great feast. Then they

[1] Mr. Meek's conclusion that the tobacco plant is indigenous to New Guinea is not held universally. The Hon. M. S. C. Smith, Commissioner for Lands, Papua, records in his diary of the Kikori expedition, 1910-11:

"Cultivated in the native gardens we found sweet potatoes, taro, yams, sugar-cane, bananas, betel-nut, and ginger, the last-named cultivated as a medicine. Maize is unknown. No coconut trees were seen on the whole trip until we reached the lower waters of the Kikori River, nor are there any mango trees or tapioca. The natives grow a green vegetable, the leaves of which they boil in bamboos. It makes a very good substitute for cabbage and appears to contain a lot of vegetable oil. Tobacco is cultivated in every native garden, which might lead one to suppose that it was indigenous; the name, however, tends to show that it is an introduced plant. It is universally called "suku" by the bushmen, which is evidently derived from "kuku," the coastal name. In one of the gardens on the head-waters of the Kikori I found a kava plant (*Macropiper methysticum*), although I saw no evidence of the manufacture of the beverage."—EDITOR.

hang it up over smoke fires and dry it in that way, but the ordinary way of using tobacco is for the native to take a green leaf from the tobacco shrub and bruise it and then throw it on hot coals until it is dry, and then shred it and smoke it in a bamboo pipe. Fresh tobacco prepared in this way is not at all unpleasant to smoke, and my Malay servant used to make me quite decent cigars of native tobacco.

These hill tribes of New Guinea have a very quick method of making a fire. They cut a species of lawyer cane into about three-feet lengths and twist it into rings, of which they will carry some half-dozen or so on each arm. These lengths of vine are called "New Guinea matches." When a native wishes to make a fire he takes from his arm one of these rings and then chooses a bit of very dry wood which he splits half way down. His next step is to make a tinder of a little shred of tapa cloth, which he puts into the slit of the wood. The piece of wood is then laid on the ground and steadied with the native's foot, and the length of dried vine passed under it, and drawn very quickly to and fro. The friction generates enough heat to set the tapa tinder aflame in a very few seconds.[1]

---

[1] I have already quoted in a previous footnote from the observations of the Hon. M. S. C. Smith on the hill tribes in the Kikori division. His record of this method of fire-making (which is far more generally known among the natives than he supposed) is as follows—

"Their method of making fire is superior to the usual Papuan

NATIVE WOMEN WITH TOBACCO PIPES.

The hill tribes of New Guinea are conspicuously honest, and their social lives are very decent. Those who wish to get on well with the mountain tribes must respect their womenfolk. Any illicit interference with them would be sternly resented. But if a white man wins the favourable regard of the natives he can obtain a wife, either as a present or in exchange for gifts on his part. But it is distinctly understood that the woman is to be his wife, not a temporary concubine. A great deal of the trouble with natives in Papua is due to misunderstandings over the native women. One particularly grave mistake made by white men in some instances is to attempt to interfere with the women-carriers whom he has engaged. For some reason, which I do not quite understand, that is looked upon with particular resentment by the natives.

The usual system of marriage is by purchase, and among these hill tribes it seems to work very well. There is a tendency—hardly wise in my opinion—

---

system. They get a piece of dry, soft wood, split one end and insert a piece of tapa cloth, then, taking a piece of cane which they carry twisted round their waists, they place it under the wood, on which they stand. Grasping each an end of the cane, they pull it backwards and forwards vigorously; when it has eaten half way through the wood to the tapa cloth the heat generated is so great that the cloth smoulders and is blown into flame. The whole process is accomplished in ten or fifteen seconds. I am informed that certain natives of the Main Range about Kagi adopt this system also; if so, it is interesting as probably showing some connexion between them."—EDITOR.

on the part of some British officials in Papua to set their faces against the native marriage customs. Thus I notice a resident magistrate recently reporting to his government—

"Perhaps one of the most repugnant of these native laws or customs is the 'Maoheni,' or the marriage betrothal contract, which absolutely relegates the native woman to the status of a mere chattel. A native woman or girl has no voice in the selection of her partner, and the matter is simply one of purchase. Children just born are in innumerable instances betrothed, and payment made to the family of the female infant, and, no matter how much the girl dislikes her affianced husband when she attains marriageable age, she cannot protest. When not betrothed in infancy, the father of a young man selects a wife for his son, and approaches the parents of the girl with the payment. If the payment is accepted, the girl takes up her abode in her husband's house, and in many instances she may never have seen or spoken to that husband before entering his home. She is never consulted as to her likes or willingness.

"Needless to say, numbers of these forced marriages turn out unhappily, and inevitably end in separation. Separation or divorce—it is more a divorce, as they seldom become reunited—does not free the woman from bondage or guardianship all her life. In spite of the separation, she still belongs to her husband until another man makes him sufficient payment, when she

THE KISS, PAPUA.

thereupon passes to the new man's control and authority. In the case of a widow, the deceased husband's family collect the payment from the next suitor for her in marriage. In some tribes the community collects the payment in the case of widows.

"There is no recognition in the native laws or customs of the right of a woman to attain majority, but amongst the more civilised natives of the division we are gradually placing the woman in a position to emancipate herself from a condition which is distasteful and objectionable to her, so she will be free to choose her own partner in life. Experience in this shows that the emancipation of the woman in this respect has no disastrous effect on native family life. It is, without a doubt, quite the other way, and the woman having the right to refuse the man selected for her, and marry the man of her affections and choice, enters into a contented and happy partnership. During the year, I have had several voluntary complaints from young girls to the effect that they were being forced by their parents to marry men whom they disliked and did not wish to marry, and I have prevented these marriages taking place, and arranged that the girls should follow the dictates of their own hearts, irrespective of the buying and selling propensities of their parents, and in every instance the result has been most gratifying. As civilisation and education spreads, it will be found that the native woman's endeavours will tend towards a higher and more self-respecting position than that of a chattel to be bought and sold at pleasure, and she will learn to understand the freedom that has come to her, and be careful not to abuse its privileges. It may be contended that this emancipation of the native woman will tend to promote lax morality amongst the women, but to my mind the danger of this is not great, for with the influence and teachings of our Christian Missions any tendency in this respect is likely to be overcome."

It is interesting to hear of this dawn of progressive ideas among the Papuan women. But the balance of opinion among those who know the South Sea Islands best is that the native customs, such as they are, represent the standard of morality naturally attainable in that particular district, and undue interference with them usually leads to retrogression rather than betterment. Marriage by purchase offends European sentiment: but it seems to work satisfactorily enough in practice in the South Seas. One has more sympathy with the efforts of the Government to better the conditions of the widows. There has never been in Papua the custom of immolating a woman on the death of her husband. But the bereaved widow has an uncomfortable time by native custom. To give an instance from one of the visiting magistrate's reports:

"At Ifu village I heard that a widow in mourning had been shut up in her house for over one year, and had never once been outside during that time. I interviewed her mother and told her that the widow was to be allowed out of the house at once. The unfortunate girl was almost blind from the effects of the smoke on her eyes. Informed the people that the system of confining widows in this manner was not a good one and was to discontinue, and that any person who insulted or laughed to scorn any widow for not going into retirement for a year in the house of the deceased husband would be punished. The practice is a bad one, inasmuch as the widow is compelled to live alone in the house and never move out until some man wishes to marry her, and only then is she released. If the woman is old or unattractive, it simply means imprisonment for life, as no one wishes to marry her."

At Bwoidunna I made a very fine collection of lepidoptera. I made discoveries of several new *Delias*. Just before my coming the forest had been on fire, and there was a great deal of dead timber lying around. I got some of my boys to cut wood during the day as materials for bonfires. At night these great fires were lit and attracted great numbers of moths. It was from my experience of the fine moths obtained in that way that I decided afterwards to bring acetylene lamps as part of my outfit for hill expeditions so as to collect by night.

I stayed here some three months, keeping in touch with civilisation once a month by sending down for my mails to Manna Manna Mission Station. Towards the end of my stay I sent the Malay servant who accompanied me to a spot higher up on the mountains, with two or three of my collecting boys, to see if any new butterflies were to be caught at a higher elevation. He did not come back at the expected time, so I left my camp standing and went down to the coast to dispatch my collections.

What a pity it is there are so many thousands of languages in New Guinea which are only of use within a few miles! Coming along from Okuma I had the chief of the village as guide, and coming to a branch track I asked him where it went to. He gave me the name of the place (which I forget), and made a noise of no sense, like a hen cackling, to make me understand that they spoke a language he did not know.

These Papuans, by the way, would badly shock the "Native Birds Protection Society." They are worse than any ladies for feathers. They skin the magnificent Killolo and hang it down their backs. The long-tailed Birds of Paradise, of both species, are used as the crowning piece of an elaborate head-dress. They are known as "Finema" (the big one) and "Maga" (the smaller one), though when speaking of them both they call them "Quiva." The bower birds are made into a very fine head-dress, every feather being tied separately. They are called "Goroworo." The very handsome long-tailed red parroquet is also plucked and mounted on strings. It is called "Sisi." Of

A CHEERFUL LADY, PAPUA.

the other, smaller red parroquet, only the tail feathers are used. It is called " Asifa." I counted the centre tail feathers of one chief's head-dress, and found it took twenty-three birds to make.

My Natural History notes on this district (Inland New Guinea, near the head of the Aroa River, 1903), begin with a note on the very curious Saturnid found there, high on the hills, which spins its web on communal lines. A number join together to make a huge web which is sometimes two feet and more across. The natives eat the *pupæ* of this moth, and use the web (which somewhat resembles cloth), as a head-dress to keep out the rain. It is perfectly water-tight. I bred about a dozen of these Saturnids.[1] The male hatched out a bright ochraceous tawny and the female a dull drab brown.

The place was simply astonishing as regards the number of species of moths. It was difficult to take two insects of the same species consecutively, any one night. Of the purple-shouldered *Papilio weiskei* I took a very large number.

There were, I soon found, several distinct species of *Ornithoptera*: the *goliath* and *meridionalis*, then two species apparently perfectly distinct of the form that resembles *cassandra*. We took at first two of one and one of the other, and what I took for a female of the latter resembling almost exactly the female of *goliath*. One species has four small gold

[1] The Saturnid is *Opodiphthera sciron*, Westw. (1881).—K. J.

spots on the edge of the underwing, also a long gold spot near the base of the underwing, and has a longer and narrower fore-wing than the other species; also the space of black between the golden bars is narrower. The hind-wing is very much brighter, being of a bright satiny green while the other is shaded with black. There is also a big difference in the shape of the hind-wing, the latter being larger and more angular, while the other seems perfectly round.

Then I found what I took for a fifth species of *Ornithoptera*.[1] It was very small, about the same size as *Paradisea* but almost identical, so far as my recollection went, with *richmondia*. It had blue-tinted green hind-wings, the green vein in fore-wing was completely absent, and it was altogether different from the others. I only got the one specimen. It was brought to me by one of my boys (not a collector) wrapped up in a green leaf. It was raining hard and he had to swim a big river with it. It was a newly hatched specimen.

All the butterflies are found near the creeks. I suppose it is because it is warmer at night there. I sent collectors up the mountain until I was tired; they never got anything. It was in the gullies and creeks the butterflies were found. The *Delias* fly up and down the creeks about twelve feet off the ground and

---

[1] These specimens belong to *Papilio priamus poseidon*, Doubl (1847), which varies very much in both sexes.—K. J.

until I found out how to catch them we got very few.
The successful lure was to fix an old specimen on a
leaf in the sun with wings outspread; the others
could not resist that. It was like attracting parrots
with a wounded one of their number. The purple-
shouldered *Papilio* we got only in one place, at a
soakage close to the creek bank. The *Delias*, I found,
all feed on mistletoe as caterpillars. It seems all of
one kind, but I fancy that, as it grows on the different
trees, so it takes slightly different characteristics and
forms the food-plant of the several butterflies.

Regarding birds I noticed that the *Pitta* found in
mountains is different from the red-breasted Eastern
Coast species (*Pitta loriae*),[1] not being so big and
having chestnut at the back of the neck and more
grey in its cap. I found at Bwoidunna a little tree-
bird, similar to a wren, with long flat beak, blue
cap, dirty white throat and belly, and chestnut back
(*Iodopsis wallacei*). There was also a duck with a
curious stiff tail,[2] with mottled markings, and a cuckoo
almost exactly similar to the English cuckoo. Yet
another bird new to me was neither a *Pitta* nor a
thrush, but had a thick beak somewhat similar to
a finch, and was more like a Cardinal bird. It had a

[1] The *Pitta* is a new form of *P. mackloti* just described by Mr. Rothschild and myself.—E. H.
[2] This duck is the rare *Salvadorina waiginensis*, Rothsch. & Hart. The cuckoo is *Cuculus optatus*, Gould, a bird which breeds in Eastern Siberia and passes the winter in Australia and New Guinea.

sage-green back, dirty whitish belly, chestnut crest and yellow throat. This is the *Pachycephala gamblei* of Mr. Rothschild. It stops on the tops of the mountains at the same altitude as the long-crested bower-bird and the long-tailed Bird of Paradise. Another ground bird I found seemed to be a cross between a land-rail and a *Pitta*, had very small wings, which it does not use (at least one of my men ran after one, until it hid in a deep hole between stones, and it never attempted to fly). It is of chestnut colour, with a darkish back, and blackish wings with light stripes across. The tail in both specimens was very ragged, which is a peculiarity of the species.[1]

Among mammals I noticed two kinds of climbing wallaby, both almost exactly alike, excepting one had a round head similar to the Australian native bear (koala), and the other had a long prominent shiny nose absent in the other. The difference in the skull was not so much as I should have thought from the difference in the outside features. I noted also what can only be described as a giant rat. It was two feet four inches long (or was before it was skinned). It is big as a Cuscus. I found also a midget black female wallaby, which only measured two feet two inches long, including its tail. It was full-grown, as it had a young one in its pouch.

While I was on the coast my Malay man came down

[1] This peculiar bird belongs to the family of the Rails, and is called *Rallicula forbesi*.—E. H.

bringing several species of butterflies which I had never seen, but of which I had had descriptions. I decided therefore to make another expedition to this locality later on. But meanwhile I went to Port Moresby and sent my collections away.

At that time there was a bad outbreak of measles along the coast. Measles, when first introduced into savage countries, is almost as deadly as small-pox would be amongst Europeans. I got my collectors away from the coast apparently all right, but by the time I got them up to Okuma one case of measles developed among the collecting boys. I made the patient as comfortable as I could, and left him camped there and pushed on with the rest of my carriers beyond Bwoidunna. The elevation there was great, and the weather at the time, which was the end of May, was bitterly cold. I pitched camp and soon got a very fine collection indeed.

Regarding birds, I obtained a bird which had been reported to me as to be found in the locality and called Weiske's nightjar. From the first I thought that it could not be a true nightjar or I should have got it before, as the ordinary nightjar (*Caprimulgus macrurus*) is the easiest of all night-birds to get. When I got a specimen I think my doubts were justified. This bird camps about four feet off the ground and makes a nest of small twigs similar to that of a *Podargus*, and seems, therefore, not to be a true nightjar. They range in colour from bright red to dark brown, almost black, with three strips of white-marked feathers down the breast. It was difficult to determine the sex of these birds by their plumage. I skinned many of them myself, also separated them by sexes, but there was nothing to go by in the plumage. I got deep brown males and females, likewise red ones of both sexes.[1]

Among other birds new to me was a pair in which the male was jet black with a metallic patch over each eye and a little tuft of feathers similar to that of the "*Sexpennis*" over the beak. The female was of sage-green colour; both have slight wattles along the inner edge of the beak. I took them to be some kind of Bird of Paradise.[2] There were also two specimens of a pure black *Pitta*, and a big black owl that came from a very high altitude.[3] Yet another bird new to me was a big ground pigeon. It was like a goura, but only the size of a bantam. It had a peculiar head, nostril well out to the end of the beak, and above that a flat space an inch long and half-an-inch wide, of slaty-milk colour; then about the ears it was sparsely feathered, with dark red skin, similar to

[1] This night-bird is not a true Goatsucker or *Caprimulgus*, as Mr. Meek, quite correctly, surmised. It belongs to the genus *Aegotheles*, of the family *Podargidae*, and has been named *Aegotheles insignis pulcher*, from a specimen collected by Mr. Weiske. The variations of plumage are described in *Nov. Zool.*, 1907, p. 456.—E. H.

[2] This is the *Loria loriae*, a small Bird of Paradise, confined to the mountains of New Guinea.—E. H.

[3] *Mellopitta lugubris* and *Strix tenebricosa*.—E. H.

a turkey, and on the head was a crest similar to that of the common goura, but smaller in proportion to the size of the bird. It had a black velvety face which changed abruptly to grey, chestnut-red belly, metallic blue-black tail. The wings were olive brown. This bird makes no nest, but lays on the ground one egg of dark creamy-white and small in proportion to the size of the bird.

Yet another new bird was somewhat similar to the English missel-thrush, but smaller and less distinctly marked. The male of this was black. There was also a black-and-white flycatcher, male and female alike, with long black feathers in the throat, that I had not seen before.

But I might go on for many pages recording interesting and rare birds and insects that I encountered at this spot for the first time. Every day seemed to bring its thrill. I saw in my mind catalogues in England swelling with discoveries. In the middle of it all came disaster.

It was too cold there; the boys could not stand it; they were shivering all the nights. When it was raining or foggy it was not so bad, but on clear nights the cold was piercing. I think we were about as far inland as anyone had gone to collect systematically; yet we were nothing like as far inland or as high as one could go. But the weather to tropical natives was impossible. Suddenly every one of the party with the exception of three went down with the

K

measles—a Kanaka and a New Guinea boy with myself alone escaping.

I made a resolute effort to nurse my boys back to health, for the collecting was promising to be sensational. The day the measles broke out, some of the natives of the district who were collecting for me had brought in the butterfly which I took at first to be the *Troides goliath*, but which on examination proved to be an entirely new species, which has been called the *Troides chimæra*. It was a female specimen. (Among the *Troides* the females are almost the same in colour, but the males differ very widely.) In this particular butterfly the female has a hairy body, probably because of the intense cold of the mountains in which she has her habitat. No other species of *Troides* or *Ornithoptera* that I know of has a hairy body.

It was particularly vexing to me that just after this important discovery, and whilst the collecting generally was so very promising, I had to face the alternative of staying where I was, and thus almost certainly sacrificing the lives of my boys, or of returning to the coast. One by one the sufferers from measles contracted pneumonia. As each one fell ill I had him isolated in a hospital tent, in the effort to prevent the spread of the disease. But all was in vain, and at last I had all who had suffered from measles very ill with pneumonia.

It was truly pitiable to hear the laboured breathing

and to see the miserable expression of the sufferers. I was torn between two desires: that of saving them and that of going on with the collecting work which gave such rich promise of new discoveries.

I suppose that the people of civilised countries will wonder that there was any doubt for a single moment in my mind, as to whether the health—and perhaps lives—of the boys should be sacrificed for the sake of collecting a few butterflies. But in the wild world, away from the ideas of civilisation, one gets what I would call not a recklessness or an indifference to human life so much as a somewhat different idea of its value. A certain work to be done seems to be a bigger consideration than human life, even one's own life. I have often during the course of my experiences been so desperately ill from fever and privation that it seemed impossible that I should go on with the work which I had in hand. The alternatives seemed to be to turn back or to die. But I do not recollect ever having turned back on account of any health-suffering of my own. But the state of these boys was so pitiable that when one of them died and the fate of the others seemed almost certain death I decided to strike camp and make for the coast. As soon as we climbed down the mountains and the climate became warmer, the boys recovered quickly. Indeed before we reached the coast the majority of them were strong enough to help in the carrying. Yet if they had been atttacked with measles in their native villages probably the majority of them would have perished.

At this high camp I had been able to stay only a fortnight, and I only collected in all 200 specimens. But almost everything I got there was new. It was certainly, from a collecting point of view, the most wonderful fortnight that I had ever had.

The natives in this district used to bring me great numbers of Birds of Paradise, which they had snared. The birds were brought bound with nooses to long sticks. One day there must have been between 150 and 200 birds in my camp of several different species. The sight was a most beautiful one. As a rule I bought the birds from the natives and released the females, keeping only the males for my collections.

Getting back to the coast I made for Port Moresby, where I paid off my boys, sent home my collections, and went on to Cooktown for a spell.

The voyage across to Cooktown was somewhat adventurous. My boat had been laid up at Manna Manna for some six or eight months, and when we got to sea we found that the seams had all sprung. I was obliged to caulk them at sea during some rather heavy weather.

CHAPTER VIII

ANOTHER TRIP TO THE SOLOMONS—AND TO THE NEW GUINEA HILL COUNTRY

AFTER a holiday spell at Cooktown I went back to Samarai to inspect my farm, which I now let to a tenant. From there I went across to the Solomons in the *Hekla*. In some cases I was fortunate enough to come upon new territory which had never been worked before, and got some new specimens, but there was no hill work to be done in the Solomons, and the hills are always best for butterflies and moths. At Gizo I did fairly well for three weeks and then made for Choiseul Island, where the natives had at this time (1903) a very bad reputation. The danger there was thought to be so great that it was not considered wise for all the party to work ashore at the same time. I established my camp on a small island off the main island, so as to be in a better position for defence in case of attack, and one of us always cruised about near the shore in a boat whilst a party was collecting on shore. The boat would have taken off the party to the island camp in case of danger threatening.

The natives of Choiseul are not only savage to strangers, but are by no means friendly among themselves. There are some tribes on the island that are in a way outcasts, and live in the bush. They are hunted down by the people who live in the villages. There is no difference that I could notice between the tribes who live in the villages and these outcasts who are driven into the bush, but the village people will not allow the bush people to settle down and make gardens. The people who live in the bush have therefore to live by hunting and fishing. I used to do a great deal of fishing for the natives with dynamite.

At Choiseul I discovered a very wonderful bird, which the Hon. Walter Rothschild names after me *Microgoura meeki*. It is a kind of crested ground-pigeon and was my best discovery so far in Natural History.

After Choiseul I made my way to Rendova Island (1904), where I stayed some six or nine weeks. Here the collecting was fairly good and I got a new specimen of *Troides* called the *Troides rubianus*, which is darker in appearance than the *Troides victoriae*. There was a strange Natural History specimen here that I encountered, but I was not able to collect for Tring Museum—a very small and very old native, covered all over with red hair. He was reputed by the natives to have already reached a fabulous age, and they stated that " he was never going to die."

After staying in the British Solomons for some eight months I sent away my collections, and went

ANOTHER TRIP TO THE SOLOMONS

on to the German Solomons, making the island of Bougainville my headquarters. At that time (1904) the Germans were using Bougainville Island as a recruiting ground for labour for their colony in New Britain, and the German law was that boats should not go to Bougainville without first entering at New Britain. Now New Britain was some 200 miles out of my track, and so I took leave of my friends the Germans to collect at Bougainville without going through the formality of entering at the Customs at New Britain. I sailed up a little river a short distance from the coast and made a clearing out of sight of the coast-line and started collecting. There I was able occasionally to see a German vessel patrolling the coast, but on no occasion was I seen.

At Bougainville I got a very handsome and big kingfisher new to me, and a waterhen or large rail. I also got two butterflies new to me, a *Papilio* and a *Charaxes*. The male of this *Charaxes* was perfectly black with just a single row of blue half-moon shaped dots inside of both wings.[1] Of the female of this species I had got two broken specimens before from Choiseul Island. The *Papilio* got at Bougainville was somewhat similiar to a previous Rendova specimen, but had more colour, especially in the hindwing. This Bougainville kingfisher had orange bill and feet, red chestnut head, blue collar, red cape, blue wings and tail, and a light brilliant blue streak on back. The

[1] A form of *Eulepis epigenes*, G. & S. (1888).—K. J.

female had an olive brown back. I got there also a fine series of *Ornithoptera victoriae* ranging from pale copper to gold and brilliant green in colour.

I came to the conclusion that those naturalists were mistaken who imagined the larvæ of the *Troides chimæra* fed on the same creeper as all other species of *Troides*, including the *victoriae* of the Solomons. The *chimæra* I found to be quite unlike any other *Ornithoptera* inasmuch as it keeps to the dense scrub tree-tops and does not hover over the second growth of old gardens as do all others. The larvæ are totally unlike any other larvæ of the same family, inasmuch as every spine has three other subsidiary spines at right angles half-way up, but has the two white marks as in the larvæ of other *Ornithoptera* with the exception of the larvæ of the *victoriae*, which have red spines with black tips, but all alike. I got a great number of the young larvæ of *T. chimæra* by squeezing eggs from females, but could find no food plant on which to rear them. There should be a new *Ornithoptera* in the mountains of the Solomons, either at Guadalcanar or Bougainville. But it is not so likely that there will be new finds on any of the other islands, as the mountains are not very high and start almost from the coast. On the before-mentioned islands there is, however, a big extent of flat country first, and the mountains are very high, and rise more gradually. In Bougainville, of course, it would be impossible to work the mountains without the aid of a large armed

ANOTHER TRIP TO THE SOLOMONS

party, and that would need the German Government's sanction. It is, however, a possible trip of the future.

Pleased with my work at the Solomon Islands I made my way back to New Guinea and Cooktown, sending forward my collections as usual and taking a spell for some three or four months.

After this trip to the Solomons I decided to obtain for the trip I contemplated to inland New Guinea a couple of savage dogs, to warn " walk-about " natives that some one was in camp. I had heard that the natives inland on the N.E. coast of Papua were very treacherous. But all South Sea Island natives are frightened of a savage dog, and these dogs proved of value in warning off intruders. But as I have said, I rested some three months.

Then when the fever of travel seized me again I decided to make an expedition to the place under the Stanley Ranges where I had found the female of the *Troides chimæra*. My purpose was in particular to discover the male of that species. As will be recalled, I had reached the spot previously from a point on the coast called Manna Manna. But now I had heard from a Cingalese native that I could get very much more easily to the same spot by taking off from the coast at a point opposite Yule Island, forty miles west from Manna Manna.

In 1905 I made my way accordingly from Samarai to Yule Island, and when I arrived at the place which had been indicated to me I left my boat in charge of a trader and hired from the natives two very large canoes, with which I made some progress up the river until I got to a camp of sandalwood getters. The chief of this camp had drays and horses, which he employed in getting his timber to the coast, and I was able to make arrangements with him to carry my stuff inland for me a full day's journey. At the end of this stage I encountered the usual trouble in regard to carriers. The men of the district near the coast would not go inland for fear of the tribes there. Previous experience had taught me how to overcome these difficulties. I left my boys in camp and then went forward alone and got a number of the people from higher up to come down and carry my gear for me. It took three days to get to the first of the mountain villages, and on this occasion I had a train of seventy carriers. It occupied all my time to keep them in meat, shooting wallaby and pigeons for their consumption. Occasionally I got a cassowary, but these birds are now becoming rare in New Guinea. What struck me as strange was that the carriers whom I had brought down from the mountains seemed quite lost on the flat country of the coast and did not know their bearings.

When I had got to the first of the mountain villages, at a height of some 2000 feet, I was obliged again to go ahead and recruit carriers for the next stage. Frankly I cannot now understand either the general stories of the savage nature of the inland tribes of British Papua, nor the objection of the coast tribes to penetrate inland, nor that of the tribes on the slopes to go higher up the mountains; for my experience of the mountain tribes was generally most favourable. In this particular district I found them on the whole singularly hospitable. Always when I arrived at a mountain village I had a pig presented to me by the chief of the village. It would have been a serious breach of good manners if I had not given a return present. The pig presented to me I usually handed over to my carriers. But on the mountains of New Guinea I do not object to a joint of pork for my own consumption. The mountain pig is a good, honest animal which is fed by the natives on potatoes and other clean food. The coast pig, on the other hand, is a scavenger, and I would never think of eating pork on the coast.

The Cingalese who had told me of the short cut from the coast to the country below the Owen Stanley Ranges proved to have been a good guide, for with comparatively little trouble I reached to a height corresponding with the spot to which I had before travelled from Manna Manna, and went past it to higher country, to a place at the Angabunga River, which flows into the St. Joseph River. I found these highlands singularly beautiful and wholesome. The gardens round the villages have their boundaries marked with croton hedges, which, with their leaves striped red and green, made a gorgeous note of colour in the landscape.

The agriculture of these people I found to be of a good type and their hospitality to strangers and among themselves is very warm.

From a collecting point of view this hill expedition was quite the best that I had yet undertaken. I made more discoveries than I could tell of among the lepidoptera. My highest camp was at an altitude of about 7000 feet, and I worked from there down to an altitude of about 5200 feet, generally in country which no white people had ever seen before. I got a good many females of the *Troides chimæra*, which the natives were accustomed to shoot for me with their bows and arrows. They captured specimens, too, with nets made most ingeniously with spiders' webs.

The manner of making these nets was this. With a very fine forked stick the native would make something like the framework of a tennis racquet. This he would run again and again through and through the strong web spun by the big yellow spider common in the bush there. Having thus got some web across the net, I have sometimes seen the natives get a big, fat spider on to the frame, then shake him off. As he tried to climb up they would keep twisting the frame and shaking it slightly to prevent him ever reaching it. Thus the spider was made to spin fresh strands for the net. I have never heard of these nets being used for catching fish, as has been reported by one traveller. *That*, I should say, is a fairy tale, unless it were for prawns or very small fish. A native left a very large net similar to what I have described outside my camp one day. For a night it was standing in the rain, and it was completely spoilt as far as butterfly-catching went, for all the stickiness had gone out of the web and it had become as though it were glazed over. Water having that effect on this spider web I cannot think of these web-nets as possible for fish-catching. My own view is that the spider-web nets were originally designed by the natives as toys, or as snares for very small birds. I have seen the same sort of thing in other parts of New Guinea, especially in the Trobriand Islands.

The ingenuity of the natives in making weapons and toys is sometimes very remarkable. I recall in particular a kind of jew's harp that the children make in the Solomon Group. They get one of the big weevil beetles that infest the sago-palm roof-thatching, break off one joint of the foreleg, and in the hollow of the insect's bone put a thin twig stripped from a coco-nut leaf. As the insect with its long proboscis spins around it makes a vibrant humming against this twig.

The inland natives of New Guinea, by the way, fully sympathised with my enterprise of butterfly collecting. They put great value themselves on the beautiful feathers of various birds, weaving them into gorgeous head-dresses. If they had had any means of putting the frail wings of butterflies to decorative use they would doubtless have done so. I found them usually to be sympathetic and intelligent collectors. They, however, cannot see the use of hunting for gold.

I captured the male of the new *Ornithoptera chimæra* at last. It was a most beautiful insect, all black and gold; with three long stripes on the forewing, hind-wing semi-transparent and gold, and inclined to be tailed. It was as large as the female common *Ornithoptera* and very broad across fore-wing. I felt more pleased than if I had been left a fortune when the male specimen came in, and I astonished the successful boy with the amount of largesse he got. He had two shillings—he knew the value of English currency—two tins of English bacon and five sticks of tobacco. A fine discovery of that sort stirs the heart of a collector. He forgets hardships and troubles, and remembers only that he has given something to science, taken from Nature one more of her secrets. "A little secret!" some may say, but naturalists do not think so.

To see this insect in flight was fine. The hindwings are (when the insect is alive or fresh) almost a transparent gold, but I notice after it has been dried that the transparency somewhat disappears. I saw one flying about four or five hundred feet above the ground, and the gold hind-wings were so conspicuous

ANOTHER TRIP TO THE SOLOMONS

that it looked to have brilliant yellow tails. But I noticed that in old specimens, along the fore margin of the fore-wing the gold turns to bluish green, on account of sun or weather.

Afterwards the natives brought in four males of the common *Ornithoptera*, thus giving a standard of comparison and clearing up any doubts, and a female of the great banded *Ornithoptera chimæra*. I got one egg from her, but could not find any Aristolochia there to rear the *larva* on. Another addition to the collection here was a large "owl" butterfly, of chocolate colour. It had two large eyes on the underside of the hind-wing, and a large eye and two small ones on the top side of the hind-wing, exactly like the eyes of the "peacock" butterfly of England. It also had another similar eye in the tip of each fore-wing with a wide cream of yellow band across the fore-wing. It reminded me of the South American butterflies, but was not so large.[1]

There was yet another white butterfly found there, which seemed to be of a new genus, and several handsome day-flying moths, making six species of dayfliers not before taken by me. But the *Ornithoptera* male alone was worth coming for. It was the most handsome and largest *Ornithoptera* I had ever seen.

Still the run of good luck continued. There

---

[1] Mr. Meek found here two new species of *Morphopsis*, *M. meeki* and *M. ula*; both described in *Nov. Zool.*, 1905, pp. 454 and 456, and figured, *loc. cit.*, 1906, Pl. III.—K. J.

came in next another species of the great purple-eyed owl butterfly. This is indeed a very beautiful insect. It has two big eyes on the under-side of the hind-wing and one purple eye on the top-side of the hind-wing, and a large snow-white patch across the fore-wing, which is very wide. The day of this capture some Eleda boys came over from the head of the Aroa with many fine specimens of *Ornithoptera*. They told me they had their chief " medicine man " in the bush under the blossom trees " saying his prayers " (making " pouri-pouri ") to induce the butterflies to come. They were much more successful than my own boys; whether the butterflies were more numerous there, or whether the natives were more energetic, I could not say. But I did not give the " medicine man " any of the credit.

I have never noticed in New Guinea any birds hunting the butterflies, and I think that these gorgeous insects can have no natural enemy. If they had they would all soon be exterminated, since their colours are so striking and their powers of escape so very slight. I know of many cases in which certain species of moths are hunted regularly by birds, but I never recollect having seen a butterfly captured or hunted by a bird.

After I had got the first specimen of the male *Troides chimæra* I showed it to my native collectors, and to the natives of the district who were helping me in collecting, and after that several specimens

ANOTHER TRIP TO THE SOLOMONS

were brought to my camp by the boys. They would come to me often wrapped up with leaves in a cleft stick, and yet had been handled so delicately that they were perfect specimens. After a native had proved that he knew something of butterfly collecting I would give him a net to work with. Altogether I stayed in this district some three or four months, and I can put to the credit of the place some hundreds of new discoveries, including some very beautiful day-flying moths. There were, however, not many new birds to be discovered.

About the habits of the natives in that hilly district, I found that the people were much given to intertribal fighting as an amusement. In the village where I had my camp the natives were at loggerheads with the villages higher up, and would make expeditions to the hills with the object of killing some of their enemies. I did not notice that they were particularly anxious to collect heads, and if cannibalism were associated with these expeditions it did not come directly under my notice. I fancy that the fact that a white man was living at my village prevented the natives of the higher villages from descending upon our village for return raids. I have a suspicion that the people of our place represented that I was very powerful " magic," and took advantage of my presence among them to make raids without fear of reprisals. Certainly (as is usual where the presence of the white man was before unknown) there was a great deal of awe of my humble self. At no time during all my stay there had I trouble at all with the natives, and I was particularly gratified with the good work of the collectors.

Some observations on the methods of communication between the hill villages in high New Guinea will be interesting. The villages are built as a rule on the tops of spurs and, as it is what I have called before "switchback" country, the distance by path from one village to the next is often very great. But a kind of inter-village telephone system has been established as a means of communication. Early in the morning, while the air is very still, a crier from a village will go to a selected spot and sing out across the valley to the next village. As soon as an answering cry is received from that village, the crier will chant the news that he wishes to convey. Generally he will repeat his message twice. When the man at the other village understands fully he will sing back "koo koo koo." If he wishes the message to be repeated he will sing a single "koo." Then, perhaps, an answering message will be sent or, perhaps, the message will have to be conveyed further along to another village by the same means. I came to know about this telephone system in this way. I had heard that a man had died in a village near by, and that his death had been put down to "magic" on the part of people in the village called Farn, some three days off. The Papuans have many methods of trial for magic. In a recent trial of a native from the village on the Bartholomew Range, there was evidence of a curious custom that the natives of this place used to find out if the native had died by sorcery or not. The body is placed on a platform in the centre of the village, and a leaf placed on the breast; the feet are then pointed in the direction of a village, and the body asked if any man or woman in the village pointed at caused the death. If the leaf falls off the body, the people are sure that the person who caused the death was a native of the village pointed at; if the leaf does not fall off the body at the first attempt, the body is pointed to another village, and so on until the leaf falls—or is blown off. The natives blame almost every death to sorcery. In particular the inland people are eaten up with superstition, and any "magic" man can terrorise them into doing what he wishes.

But in this case of the accusation against the people of Farn it would seem that the charge broke down— whatever the method of trial—for within half an hour after the accusation was made I learnt that this accusation of magic against the Farn people had been conveyed to them, and that they had answered that they knew nothing at all of the man's death, and that in order to prove their good faith and innocence they would come over to the village of which he had been an inhabitant and take part there in a ceremonial dance.

If anybody is travelling in that part of New Guinea the natives will know of his arrival in a village many days before he gets there. The communications by crier are only made early in the morning, whilst the air in the valley is still. When the sun gets up and disturbs the air currents in the valleys, it does not seem to be possible for the native criers to make their voices heard across from one hill to another. I believe that operators in wireless telegraphy find this same difference—certain hours being far more favourable for carrying the sound-waves than others.

The climate in these hill districts is very cold at night but warm and genial by day. It is usual for a shower of rain to fall almost every day. My custom was to wear two suits of clothes on getting up in the morning and discard one at 10 a.m., when the sun had become fairly hot.

The food of the natives at this altitude consists in the main of sweet potatoes, bananas, cucumbers and other vegetable products, with an occasional meal of pork. The natives cook their meat by roasting. Only on the coast, or very near the coast, do the New Guinea natives make pottery. It is the custom for the men to sleep in hammocks underneath which small fires are kept burning. Whether the idea of this is to keep off insects or to keep away the damp mists I do not quite know. Perhaps both considerations enter into the custom. It is usual for all the men of a village to sleep in a large house at one end of the village, but each man would have his own house in addition, where his wife and family would live.

These hill natives are very hospitable, and welcome

visits from friendly neighbouring villages. Advantage would always be taken of these visits to hold a social dance. The village square would be decorated for the occasion with green trees and flowers. There would be dances for the men and dances for the women and athletic exercises for the young men. On the occasion of a festival of this kind a guest-house is built, big enough to accommodate the 200 or 300 people who come from the neighbouring villages. I was never quite able to understand the system on which this mutual hospitality was arranged, but the occasions for dances and festivals were the potato harvests, the yam harvests, and such other occasions.

I stayed at my camp in the district until about May 1905, and then descended to the coast to Port Moresby to send away my collections. Then I went back for a short time to finish up a collection. On this short second trip I did not get very many specimens of lepidoptera, but the natives brought me numbers of Birds of Paradise and other birds.

The natives in the hills of New Guinea are very clever at snaring birds, adopting many different methods for different kinds. One method is to make a kind of bird-lime out of the gutta-percha of the breadfruit tree. This is used for the smaller kinds of birds. For ground-birds the natives employ traps that are weighted with stones and baited with worms. The bird enters the trap to eat the worm and is crushed and killed by the falling of the stones. To snare Bower-Birds and Birds of Paradise the natives search for the playground of the bird, and then set a snare of a loop of native twine in which the bird gets entangled. In other cases Birds of Paradise are caught by a loop which is left on the bough of the tree and connected with a long piece of twine to the hunter, who is concealed in the bush near by. When the bird steps within the loop the hunter pulls the snare. Yet another way of capturing birds, such as pigeons, which fly in flocks, is to pick out a likely place on the saddle of the spur of a mountain and cut an opening there in the forest. Along this lane, which comes to be used by the birds as a means of passage, great nets are set up. Yet another method of hunting the small birds which frequent thickets is to set up funnel-shaped nets within the thicket, beating the birds towards them.

In two days near Owgarra I recollect that forty-seven male Birds of Paradise were brought to me. All arrived alive, tied by the leg with twine to sticks. There were seven or eight different species comprised in these.

There are several points of resemblance in the habits of the Birds of Paradise and the Bower-Birds in regard to setting up playgrounds during the mating season. But in no case does the Bird of Paradise have such an elaborate playground as the coastal types of Bower-Birds. There are some points of distinction between mountain and coast Bower-Birds. The mountain Bower-Birds of New Guinea have

ANOTHER TRIP TO THE SOLOMONS 151

golden crests (which are much valued by the natives for making their ceremonious head-dresses). Neither the Bower-Birds on the lower slopes, nor the Bower-Birds of the coast have these crests.

The three different kinds of Bower-Birds have entirely different habits in regard to playgrounds. The mountain Bower-Bird builds a kind of spiral staircase around a sapling. This is not very ornate. The Bower-Bird of the lower slopes of the mountains makes a very elaborate playground, which may be compared in structure to a Kaffir kraal. It is covered in with a roof, is surrounded with circular galleries, and is carpeted most elaborately with beetle wings, white snail shells and fragments of flowers. Usually a very small tree is made the centre of the bower, and the builder constructs from that as a centre his bower with interlaced vines and branches. The Bower-Bird of the coast builds a rough avenue which he paves with white snail shells. The custom of the male Bower-Bird to parade and dance in his bower in order to attract the female of the species is familiar enough and need not be described.

In hunting butterflies in this district I had noticed in regard to *Papilios* that usually you will get only the females at the blossom-trees and the males at water soakages. Very often of a particular species I would get several males at water soakages and riversides, and never get a female until my collectors tried the blossom-trees.

CHAPTER IX

SOME EXPERIENCES WITH THE NATIVES—TWO BOYS ARE MURDERED

THE next expedition I undertook had for its objective the head of the Mambaré River. As usual I had taken a short spell at Cooktown, and then I voyaged along the North-East coast of British New Guinea recruiting boys. I got some boys from Suan on the South coast, because they are such fine sailors. The other boys I got from different districts. Generally speaking my boys and I got on very well together on our various expeditions. It is a wise precaution not to take a single boy from any one village, but always to have at least a couple from the one village. They then chum up together and a boy is happier when he has a neighbour with the party. You will notice that if any of your camp boys run away it is the boys from one district who have planned to break away together, leaving the boys from other villages out of the escapade. It is, therefore, not wise to have all your boys from the one locality, because in that case they might all "give notice" together, especially if they happened to be seized with home-sickness at a time when their village was near at hand.

EXPERIENCES WITH THE NATIVES 153

I ordinarily had very little trouble in regard to the recruiting of boys, because I made it a custom to pay an advance to a boy on engaging him. This I would pay to him in native shell-money and he would leave it behind with his people.

When I was on a labour recruiting trip I would sail my boat from village to village and send boys to the shore to the villages offering the resident men so much a head for service for six months, or a year, as the case might be. The natives have different standards of payment for different types of work. The most arduous work, and the work therefore for which the highest wage is demanded, is carrying for the gold-fields. The next work in order of favour is plantation work. What the natives like most of all is the work for which I would engage them, that is to say sailing about the coast and making collections. The vagabonding nature of this work appeals to the Papuan character.

The cost of recruits varies in proportion as you can get native food or have to feed them on tinned goods. In the mountain districts where most of my collections were made I found that a hundredweight of coarse salt would feed a dozen boys for three or four months. I do not mean that the boys would eat the salt, but that was the best form of currency away from the coast (on the coast tobacco was the best small money). With that amount of salt it would be possible to buy sufficient native food for a dozen boys for the course of a collecting trip. Perhaps I would have to eke out the salt currency with fifty or sixty pounds of beads in some districts. That would be what you would call "small change." Big money would consist of knives and tomahawks. You would only pay out big money for carrying work or collecting work. Perhaps a knife would be paid as the wages for a journey, or a looking-glass, or perhaps both. The biggest money—the native Bank of England £5 note, so to speak—is pearl shell, which the inland natives value very highly.

I am often asked how I make myself understood among the natives. That I found to be easy enough on the coast, where they have come into contact with white men and the natives easily understand "pidgin" English. Where they do not you can usually find an interpreter. I speak, of course, a little of the native dialects, and get on well enough with that, helped out with "pidgin" English. A curious fact is that one cannot without great effort talk "pidgin" English to a white man, just as one never dreams of using correct English to a native.

Usually a boy is engaged for twelve months, during which time you feed him and pay him at intervals "in trade." When he gets back to his village he usually has a box full of knives and clothing and looking-glasses and native money. I made it a point, whenever a boy had proved a good servant, of giving him a bonus at the end of his term, usually a parcel

WOMEN MAKING SAGO.

of trade worth £1 or 30s. I did this in the first instance out of gratitude, but afterwards found it was also good business, for if I went back to a district at any time I found the boys anxious to work for me.

On this question of native labour the future industrial prosperity of Papua depends. Can the native be got to work steadily without compulsion? Or will it be necessary to compel him to work? Or should we do as has been done in Fiji, let the native coloured race keep to its habits of idleness, and bring in coolies from India for the plantations? All the politics of Papua hinge on these questions. The third one, however, need hardly be asked. The Australian Government would never permit the example of Fiji to be followed, and is resolved on a policy of " Papua for the Papuans." A proposal to compel the Papuan to do a little work, either for himself, for the Government, or for the planters, has also been vetoed by Australia: though it is possible that that decision may be reconsidered one day. At present the policy is to try to coax the Papuan to ways of steady industry.

The Lieut.-Governor, his Excellency Colonel Murray, has now some hope that the native sloth of the Papuan is being overcome by his greed for the white men's "trade," and he thinks that the "labour problem" might thus be solved. The official reports from various districts for 1911 give some grounds for this optimism. Here are the main facts of the reports of various officials:

KUMUSI :—When I was on the s.s. *Kia-Ora* last November, there were sixty native labourers returning to their homes, all with boxes full of trade. These men had hardly time to get to their villages before other natives began to flock in to "sign on," and in some twenty-five or thirty cases the same boys who came up by the steamer also came in, which is sure evidence that their previous term of service had not been too hard. It takes years for a native to overcome his natural antipathy to go any distance from his village, and very often, although the boy may be willing, the influence brought to bear by his parents is too strong; but when the parents and others see the boys coming back, looking healthy, strong, and in the pink of condition, with their boxes full of good things, it will be only a matter of time for the prejudice to pass away.

SOUTH-EAST DIVISION :—The Murua natives are still disinclined to "sign on" to work for Europeans, preferring the free and easy life, sailing about in canoes for the major part of their time and visiting their neighbours; but, as in foregoing years, the Government had no difficulty in getting "boys" from the local villages to work on new roads and other public works when their services were required.

EASTERN DIVISION :—The supply of native labour has been equal to the demands within the Division. The death-rate at Port Moresby and Lakekamu Goldfield has seriously interfered with the labour available

EXPERIENCES WITH THE NATIVES

for those places. The local plantations have had but little difficulty in securing the labour they require. Towards the end of the year, and with the disappearance of the dysentery epidemic at Lakekamu, a few recruits for the gold-mining industry have been coming forward, but it may be safely said that it will be many days before the native forgets the unparalleled death-rate of the Lakekamu Gold-field during the previous year.

EAST CENTRAL DIVISION :—The coastal natives, especially those around Marshall Lagoon, have a strong objection to work; but a good many of the natives from the villages at the back of Cloudy Bay may be seen working as casual labourers on several plantations. These natives seem to think that, if they enter into contract of service, they will be taken to some far-away place, and perhaps never reach their homes again. The opinion of the planters in the Cloudy Bay District is that the local natives are good workers, and give no trouble. The wages paid to plantation labourers range from 7s. 6d. to 15s. per month. They are well fed, and have comfortable houses on the plantations.

CENTRAL DIVISION :—Even with the increase of locally recruited labour, the demand seems still to be in excess of the supply, and many more labourers would be gladly welcomed by the plantations. The most of the recruits came from inland districts, the coastal natives not being willing to engage, although there is a far larger population to draw on than inland. As long as the coastal native can obtain a yam and an inch of tobacco he will not on any occasion leave his beloved platform underneath his house, where he sleeps day in and day out. But inland the conditions are different, for the bush people are learning the want of a great number of things that they did without before, and they consequently come down off their hills to work and get money to buy the things they want. The coastal people have more chances of getting tobacco, knives, etc., than the bushmen, for they have coco-nuts that can be turned into copra without very much labour, and so they remain at home.

My own opinion is that the Papuan—of this generation or the next,—will not work steadily, though he may take up, in a spasmodic fashion, some sort of work when he is anxious for "trade." But when you have "signed him on" the native boy as a worker is just what you like to make him. His character depends entirely on the character of his master. There is one certain rule, and that is that talking at the boys is bad. The natives do not mind a blow if there is a reason for the punishment, but they do not like you talking at them. Some men can never get on with the natives because they are always nagging.

After some experience with the natives a man becomes tolerant and good-humoured with regard to their little failings. If you think they are doing their best you do not worry about small faults, and learn to treat them like children, which indeed they are. But one thing you must never tolerate, that is, for a boy to tell another boy to do some task which you have entrusted to him. If you tell a boy to do a thing and he passes the task on, it is well that you should make trouble straight away. You find it also an advantage to watch your new boys and find out the man among them—there is always one—who is inclined to be what is called in Australia a " bush lawyer," that is to say, a man who wishes to make a grievance if none exists, or to exaggerate the little troubles that must occur. When you have picked upon your " bush lawyer " you may find it necessary to give him some wholesome correction. Once he has come to heel you have very little trouble with the rest.

On this expedition I had with me the two Eichhorns, whom I had engaged at Samarai, and two good Kanaka boys for shooting game, one of whom I had brought from Queensland ten years previously. From a Kumusi River camp I struck inland, and my vessel went back to Samarai with instructions to call back for me some three months later. I had great difficulty in getting carriers, as the natives had been doing a great deal of carrying work for the Government recently, and were well supplied with all trade articles. It took me a month to get about eighty miles inland and about 6000 feet high.

I had barely left the coast when my collecting boys took it into their heads to run away, the first experience of the kind I had had. Of course one must always expect that a native boy who has signed on for twelve months will find his habits of industry slacken after a fortnight or a month's time, and if he sees a chance of getting back home he will take it. My boys got it into their heads that they could reach their homes by running along the coast, and so one morning at daylight they cleared out. I went to the nearest village and offered to the chief there ample reward in trade for the arrest of the escaping boys. By the afternoon of that day the natives of the village had them all back again, and tied up to trees. I punished the ringleader and found that the boys behaved all right after that. But the work of getting inland was very laborious. It was a very unlucky trip in many respects. At the outset, the evening before leaving Samarai, some runaway boys stole my dinghey, and I had to pay fifteen pounds to get one to replace it with. Then soon after landing at Buna, I had my boys run away, as I have told. They were caught certainly before they had gone far, but it cost me thirteen tomahawks. Then the Government official whom I relied on to help me to get carriers, blocked the local carriers from carrying, so I had to do most of it with my own labour. On reaching the foot of the mountains, I had seven boys down with disease. Then, soon after arrival, two boys fell ill with pneumonia and another was disabled with paralysis in the hip joint.

However, I got to work (location Biagi, about 5000 feet high, at the head of the Mambare River: year 1906). I had barely established my camp when I encountered the first female of the *Ornithoptera alexandrae*. It was not until a year or two afterwards that I obtained a male specimen. I also got two or three specimens of the female *Troides chimœra*, but could not get a male although I saw them often. One I shot with a shot-gun, but I lost the body because of the wild nature of the country. But on the whole the insects proved so much like the Owgarra ones, that I was sorry I had ventured up so high, or so far. I captured nine or ten of the *Delias*, similar to the Owgarra ones, with little local differences. Most of the Owgarra day-flying, brightly coloured moths I found at Biagi also, with few new ones. But everything seemed to run much darker in colour at Biagi than at Owgarra. I encountered many species (one white with black border and others brown and smaller) of a sort of *Satyrid* with rounded short tails, and one specimen of the small white Nymphalid, with a deep black border.[1] I also got a good series of a moth, yellow in colour, with red irregular lines running all about on the fore-wing. It is not a high altitude insect. All the Owgarra *Delias* were found at Biagi excepting five species. I noticed that the females took

[1] The Nymphalid is a form of *Helcyra chionippe*, Feld. (1860).

a different form to those of the other side, but the females were so extremely rare, that I could only get female specimens of five or six species, and not any at all of those I wanted most particularly. I got three females of *Troides chimæra*, two or three *Morphopsis ula* and several *Morpho tenaris nivescens;* also three specimens of *Morphopsis meeki*, besides several of *albertisi*. I also got three specimens of *Charagia*. One of these specimens was rather handsome, with green fore-wings and bright rose patch on hind-wings.[1]

The Biagi moths were less disappointing than the butterflies; the number of species obtained was very much greater than in any previous collection, and the hawk moths were particularly good, with five or six species new to me.

The birds, however, like the butterflies, were disappointing at Biagi. I found nothing at all new, with the possible exception of one species of *Parotia*, which I did not collect because all Birds of Paradise were heavy in moult at the time. It is strange that altitude makes such a difference to the moulting-time of these birds, those at lower altitudes being five or six weeks earlier in moulting than those of the same species at higher levels.

I note that a close observer at the London Zoo-

---

[1] The *Charagia* is *Ch. eugyna*, R. & J. (1907). Mr. Meek obtained two males and one female; the above-mentioned specimen with red hind-wing is the female.—K. J.

logical Gardens, writing in September, comments on the moulting habits of the Birds of Paradise there:

"The majority of the birds shed their plumage at this season. The Birds of Paradise, however, are just coming into full plumage. The plumes of the males of these birds are moulted in spring and developed again in autumn, and the birds are now beginning from time to time to go through the remarkable performance known as 'display.' I watched the performance as exhibited by a specimen of the species known as Count Raggi's. The bird kept its wings stretched out horizontally with its neck bent round so that the top of its head and beak touched its perch, while the long, delicate plumes of the flanks were erected into a graceful tuft on each side, rising vertically above the wings. In this attitude it executed a kind of little dance, moving up and down and then giving a little jump on the perch and uttering a slight cry. It is curious that this display, which is, of course, connected with courtship, should be exhibited by these birds in autumn and winter, while in our European birds, as, for example, the comical little ruffs to be seen in the Waders' Aviary, it begins in spring. We can understand the coincidence of the courting spirit with the return of warmth and sunlight in the northern hemisphere, but in New Guinea and the neighbouring islands, within a few degrees of the equator, where the Paradiseidæ live, there is little difference in the temperature of the seasons. It is true that New Guinea is south of the line, so that the seasons there are the opposite of those in Europe, but the chief difference is that between the wet season and the dry, and doubtless the Birds of Paradise breed in the season which coincides with our autumn, and continue the same periodicity in this country."

Birds from Australia and the neighbouring islands seem to preserve their original habits and seasons stubbornly when transported to England. Thus the black Australian swan refuses to conform to the English climate, and hatches out its brood in the midst of the cold weather.

The birds probably would have been more plentiful for the collector at the foot of mountains instead of at that high altitude. I fancy that it is an easy matter for mountain birds to get through the various gaps and gorges in the ranges down to lower levels, when it would not be nearly so easy for the flat-country birds to ascend to higher levels. One may get mountain birds on lower slopes, but not low-country birds high up. I got one specimen of the wattled finch (male), of which I had got previously a pair at Eleda.[1]

[1] This most interesting and very rare bird is called *Eulacestoma nigropectus*, and was discovered in 1895 by Captain Armit and Mr. Guise, who made an expedition to Mount Maneao in the mountains of British New Guinea. The bird is not really a finch, but belongs to the *Laniidae* or shrikes. See *Ibis*, 1904, p. 373, and Pl. IX, where Meek's specimens are figured.—E. H.

JUNGLE, HILL COUNTRY, PAPUA.

Thus the collecting, whilst not very good, was fair. But the country was rather difficult. In that hill country the ground on which you walk is really a false turf, formed by lichens growing on the interlaced upper roots of the trees. As you walk through the forest you may sink through this and come to a kind of irregular underground cavern between the true and the false surfaces of the ground. If a bird or a butterfly or an animal is shot and falls through the false surface, it is impossible of recovery. Walking on that false surface, which quaked like a bog all the time, was not comfortable. Altogether I penetrated on this occasion up to a height of some 8000 feet. The climbing was not quite so difficult on the north side as it had been on the south side of the Owen Stanley Ranges. There were no foothills, but the flat country ran up to the edge of the great mountains.

On this expedition I was unfortunate enough to lose a couple of boys. I had brought altogether eighteen with me, and I had established two camps, one of them on a higher level, which was intended mainly as a food-collecting camp. Between this higher camp and my main camp, and also between the main camp and the coast, I kept up fairly constant communication by boys, who brought stores up from the coast and native food down from the high camp. One day, either by design or by coincidence, a simultaneous attack was made by the hill natives on my boys travelling up; and by coast natives on my boys travelling down. In both cases the goods that the boys were carrying were stolen. Of the three boys I sent down to the coast one was killed outright, another was wounded, and left for dead, but the third escaped. The wounded boy had some cunning. He was hit twice as he was crossing a creek, and fell down in the water, and was taken downstream by the current, shamming to be dead, and thus saving his life. One of my boys was killed by natives from the Kokoda district only about half a mile from a Government station. Indeed, my first news of the outrage came in a letter from the resident magistrate :—

"I regret to have to inform you that three of your boys—KANOWINI, TAUEOKO, and NABUDIGA, were attacked yesterday morning by two (presumably) Ausembo men. NABUDIGA was murdered, but of the other two, one escaped unhurt and the other was wounded. He is having his wounds dressed here, but they do not appear serious. Every effort will be made to arrest the murderers. Their swags are said to have been also stolen.

"I must request that you favour me with these boys' agreements, so that I may advise the death of the one, and must ask you to be good enough to send me the wages due to the deceased. The other two boys you will have to keep at hand, as they will be required as witnesses later."

PAPUAN POLICE BOYS.

EXPERIENCES WITH THE NATIVES

To this I replied rather sharply—being angry that a boy should have been killed so close to the Government station—telling of the other outrage by the hillmen, and stating that I intended, failing Government action, to take the matter of punishment into my own hands. To this I had the following reply:—

"I beg to acknowledge the receipt of your letter of the 13th inst., reporting attacks on your party by the Isurava natives. This matter will have my immediate attention, and I hope to be able to come up to your camp at the earliest possible moment. In the meantime I am sending two police, who have instructions to remain with you until further orders.

"I must beg that you do not take any irresponsible action with regard to punishment of the marauders, although, of course, should you be attacked you are perfectly entitled to defend yourself. If your property is obtainable, by all means recover it, but should it have been removed to the native villages, or should the attempt to recover it bring you into collision with natives, its recovery must await my presence. The police will only act in emergency, and for the moment are sent for your protection."

The native police sent up did not prove of much use. On April 17th, a boy whom I suspected of being implicated in the murder on the hills, strolled into my camp with some others, and I signed to the two native police (sent to me for "protection") to catch him: they made a good try, but he was too strong for them and bolted away in safety. On the 18th, the assistant magistrate appeared on the scene; I persuaded him to send up his six native police (all he had) to go with my boys to rescue my property. The party returned, bringing back a big drying box and a few birds' skins, spoilt by rain, and what was left of a clock lamp. On the way back, the boys found in one of the houses of a village they passed through, suspended from the roof, the bone of the fore-arm of my murdered boy. This apparently had been put there as a token of contempt for the Government, or as a challenge.

After these murders the natives around continued to be troublesome. The collecting was good, but the natives made it practically impossible for me to stay there any longer. Just as I had been driven from a good ground before by disease, on this occasion I had to give way to the ferocity of the natives, and to turn my face towards the coast. From Samarai I sent forward the collection that I had made and then made my way to Cooktown and to Cairns, where I took a spell.

I had in mind an expedition to the north-east coast next, and I wrote to the Tring Museum authorities—

" If you like I'm willing to have a try for a collection on the north-east coast, going inland as far as I deem it safe, but I can give no guarantee as to what altitude I may be able to reach; that would entirely depend on how I found the natives. They bear rather a bad reputation in those parts; being given to such playful practices (when they make a prisoner) as cutting off a man's leg and tying it up again to prevent his bleeding to death, and eating him a bit at a time. I think it quite likely, though, that I might make a good collection there, especially if I could manage to encounter a decent crowd of natives to stop with. When I speak of the north-east coast I do not, of course, mean east of Cape Nelson. That would indeed be an easy contract. I mean anywhere between Cape Nelson and the German boundary.

"In Australia I see that the Commonwealth are trying to establish state control of liquor in New Guinea. I should be glad if it proves true. It is mostly grog that has given New Guinea such a bad name, and the fever gets blamed for its work."

I had designed to complete a collection in the Solomons before the end of the year (1906), but my two South Sea shooting boys left me without their wages, rather than complete their agreement, and all my skilled boys were disposed to clear out. This last trip to the mountains had rather got on their nerves, and it was quite natural that they longed for a spell, especially as they had good cheques to spend. I made up my mind therefore to sell out in Cooktown and to go down to the cattle stations outside Rockhampton, until the winter was over, and take a trip home early the next year; returning later to complete my Solomon Islands collections. But that intention was not carried out. In 1907 I was again on the trail.

CHAPTER X

COLLECTING ON THE GIRIWA RIVER

DURING my spell in Australia I was being urged by the Tring Museum authorities to undertake expeditions to certain inland places of the Solomon Group. But I was rather reluctant to undertake these, as the financial inducements offered did not at first seem to me to be sufficient for the great expense that such expeditions would involve, and the serious risks that would be incidental to their carrying out. My last trip to the inland part of New Guinea had involved me in some financial loss, as the payments made to me were by results, and the murder of my two boys and the hostility generally of the natives had made it necessary for me to abandon a promising field, unless I had been prepared to take serious risks, not so much with my own life as with the lives of my followers.

I had a long correspondence with the Tring Museum on this point of expense. I pointed out that I was willing to complete the insect exploration of the Solomons, visiting San Christoval, Malaita, inland Ysabel, inland Guadalcanar, Rossel Island, and then go to Santa Cruz and New Hebrides. I was prepared also to penetrate into the Charles Louis Mountains

COLLECTING ON THE GIRIWA RIVER

in Dutch New Guinea to collect, but I considered it would cost a lot of money.

Finally, everything was arranged satisfactorily, Mr. Rothschild behaving, as usual, generously, and I planned to go up the N.E. coast of Papua and go inland from Oro Bay or Mosquito Islands, trying for new *Ornithoptera*. Then, after doing the Solomons and Santa Cruz, I designed to go inland up the head of the St. Joseph River again and camp at six and seven thousand feet. I made all arrangements to stay away two years, and two new men were engaged for that period.

I bought the *Shamrock*, quite the most ambitious vessel I had yet owned. She cost me some £750. I altered her rig from that of a schooner to that of a ketch. Early in 1908 I left Thursday Island for Port Moresby, where I recruited some boys as collectors, and then went up the north-east coast, making a small collection at Collingwood Bay on my way up.

I stayed about fifteen days at Collingwood Bay, about a mile up the Kimuta River, and did not get anything to make it worth while staying longer. I set nearly a thousand insects and there were about seventy birds skinned. Among lepidoptera I was surprised to get several insects which I had thought only occurred in the mountain districts.

From Collingwood Bay I made my way to Ora Bay, where I planned to make the next collection.

It is only twenty miles or less from the place where I got the female *Troides alexandrae*, and I anticipated getting that species there also. At Oro Bay the natives had been very little touched by white civilisation at that time (1907), and were more willing to work therefore to procure trade goods.

I intended to try breeding the *Troides* if possible, as it was easy to get the food plant for them on the low lands. I stayed at Oro Bay and in the vicinity about four days. I went inland from there but saw nothing worth staying for, as the country seemed to be all grass or undergrowth from old gardens. There was virgin forest on the tops of the hills, but as there was no chance of getting the long-winged *Troides* there, I passed on.

When I got to the Kumusi River again I made for the district from which I had been obliged to turn back previously. I had the misfortune at the outset to lose one of my white employees. He died rather suddenly of malarial fever and sleeplessness. He was completely off his head for three days, and was seeing motor cars, railway trains, children riding on clouds and the like. He began to be delirious on Monday morning and died on Wednesday night.

I also was on the sick list at the same time, being laid up with sores under the feet. They start with a violent itching, then small blisters form which quickly enlarge into big sores and prevent one from walking. Following that I had a bad attack of fever. It was

COLLECTING ON THE GIRIWA RIVER

very prevalent in my camp on this trip. Almost the whole time I had five or six men down. The New Guinea boys got it as badly as the others. Both my two white assistants also suffered from sores on the legs.

Getting to a position under the Owen Stanley Ranges I found the collecting very fair, and I was greatly rejoiced at last when I obtained the first male specimen of the *Troides alexandrae*. In sending it home, I wrote to Dr. Jordan of the Tring Museum, suggesting to him that since this was the most important new discovery I had yet made among lepidoptera, it should be named after the Hon. Walter Rothschild, but this Mr. Rothschild would not agree to, and it was named *Troides alexandrae* on account of its similarity to the *Troides victoriae*. On the occasion of this visit to the district I got on fairly well with the natives, but the collections on the whole were somewhat disappointing. I stayed there about three months, which was my usual stay for an inland collecting place. During that time I obtained several specimens of the long-winged *Troides alexandrae*, which measured eleven inches across the wings and were larger than the *chimæra*.

They fly very high, I noted. I also obtained about two dozen larvæ of this *Troides*. These larvæ varied considerably. The spines in some were all blood-red, with a white saddle and one spine on each side white and tipped with red. Others had spines of orange colour tipped with black and, lower, two rows of pure black. They had eight rows of very long spines, very similar to the larvæ of the *Troides victoriae* from the Solomons. The pupæ seemed, however, to be no larger than those of the common ones. They feed on an entirely different vine to other butterflies.[1] I found the first larvæ by accident the first day I reached the hills, and before, even, my camp was made. To my great joy one of the larvæ hatched out a male of a light, bright blue colour (almost electric-blue), somewhat similar to the *caelestis* of St. Aignan, with black markings.

I measured a larva of this *Troides* and it measured five inches, when lying along the vine of the food plant. This was larger than any larvæ of *Attacus hercules* that I had seen. These larvæ are very beautiful. The combination of jet velvety black with light ruby spines and broad cream-coloured band across the middle of the body makes a striking contrast. Soon I had *Troides alexandrae* in all stages from the egg to the butterfly. It was a fortunate thing I discovered the larvæ so early. It was entirely by accident. I was out looking for a suitable place for a camp, and sat down on a log, when my eye was arrested by seeing a *Troides* larva on a leaf, just about to change its skin. After that, of course, things were

[1] Mr. Meek sent some leaves of the food-plant; the authorities at Kew Gardens have examined them and pronounce them to belong to an unknown species of *Aristolochia*.—K. J.

easy, for I was able to show the natives what I wanted and get them to collect the particular larvæ.

Butterfly breeding, by the way, is quite necessary for the collector who wishes to obtain really good specimens for museums. Having discovered a new butterfly, his next step is to search the district for its larvæ and pupæ. Experience guides you as to the likely places to search. Each different species of butterfly has usually a distinguishable difference in its larvæ and pupæ. Whilst I was at this camp I found the natives fairly diligent at collecting larvæ and pupæ, as well as butterflies for me. Of the common *Troides* I got considerably over a hundred pupæ from the natives. For the good pupæ I paid looking-glasses, knives, shirts, etc., but good ones were hard to get. The larvæ were much easier to obtain, but very delicate to rear, and only a small percentage could be brought to the butterfly stage. The advantage of breeding as compared with catching the butterflies is, first, that you secure perfect specimens, and second, that you have a chance of securing now and again a " sport."

At this place I also bred two specimens of the *Papilio laglaizei*, which mimicks the moth *Alcidis* and of which I had obtained one before at Lower Biagi and another from the Lower Aroa, besides several at Milne Bay.

The birds here were disappointing. The best thing captured was a large black-and-white-breasted and black-backed falcon (which I shot with a rifle), and a goshawk of the same species that another collector had got at Buburi.[1]

On that trip to the Giriwa River I secured from the natives a small stone image which was evidently a relic of a prehistoric race. I had noticed this image in one of the villages and was anxious to obtain it to send to Europe as a curio. The natives were reluctant to part with it, but finally yielded to the temptation of an offer of two axes, but after the bargain had been struck and when one of my boys was carrying away the image, the natives seemed to be seized with some regret. To leave them thoroughly satisfied I was obliged to give them some red turkey cloth in addition to the axes.

The story they told me of the image was this: that a very, very old man, a man of a time so far remote that they could not recollect his name, a solitary man who had no wife and no children, having outlived all his kinsfolk, had brought this image up from the

---

[1] The so-called falcon is the rare *Machaerorhamphus alcinus*, with a peculiar compressed bill. It is said to be crepuscular in its habits and to catch, among other prey, bats in the evening. The goshawk is the equally rare *Erythrotriorchis doriae*, only known from New Guinea. Other rare birds obtained on the Kumasi River are: A quail, *Synoicus plumbeus*, Salvadori; a strange cuckoo, *Rhamphomantis megarhynchus* (or an allied form); a new flycatcher, *Machaerirhynchus flaviventer novus*; a new form of *Graucalus*, named after Mr. Meek; a new shrike, *Pinarolestes* and others, which will be fully discussed in a paper in the *Nov Zool.*—E. H.

river one day when he had gone there for drinking water. The old man had seen the image at the bottom of the river and had brought it to the village. It was a rough image of a man—a little suggestive of the Buddha images of Asia, with the hands crossed on the belly.

The image had been installed in a place of honour in the village, and was associated by the natives in some way with ideas of fruitfulness. They would place it in a garden for a while in order to get a good taro or yam crop. Several images of this kind have been discovered in the hill villages of New Guinea. They are sharply different from the obscene images that may be found sometimes on the coast. From the waist-line downwards these prehistoric images are not shaped in any way. On the coast, carvings in wood in the shape of men, mostly of a very indecent character, are common, but not carvings in stone. Among the hill tribes of the present day the art of carving is unknown, either in wood or in stone. Clearly this stone image which I had secured, and others of the same type, are relics of an older people.

There are also found in the hill villages of New Guinea carvings of birds with snakes' heads. As I have said, the natives of to-day have no idea of working in stone, except for the rough fashioning of clubs.

Leaving the Giriwa River I marched to the coast at Buna Bay, and then embarked on the *Shamrock* and set sail for Samarai, which I reached safely on a date in October 1907. Scarcely had I arrived when a great gale came on. Afterwards news came in of some ten vessels being blown ashore in different places during this gale, some totally wrecked. My fortunate star must have been in the ascendant, for, though I anchored for one night at East Cape, I had not remained at anchor among the reefs at nighttime between East Cape and Samarai. If I had done so I would have encountered the gale. As soon as I had anchored at Samarai the wind started. Two vessels were totally wrecked at East Cape where I had anchored, one of which was my old vessel, the *Calliope*. After this experience I decided always to keep a white man on my vessel, otherwise there was too much anxiety for one man, as in dirty weather it was necessary for me to keep on deck both day and night.

At Samarai I prepared for another visit to the Solomons. It was my intention to go inland on Guadalcanar to the mountain country, because I had much more faith in that place than any other island. The trip, I knew, would involve a good deal of risk, as there had been several murders reported from that island recently. But I was fairly confident of keeping my skull unbroken with proper precautions against treachery. After my return from the Solomons, if all went well, I designed to make another collection at Ausembo, about sixty miles inland from my camp on the Giriwa River. I am almost sure there is a form of *T. goliath* to be found there.

I have had it described to me by the natives, and one of my collectors told me once that he saw one. *Troides alexandrae* does not occur farther inland than about twenty miles, and it is only after crossing the Kumusi some forty miles' distance from the coast that one can reckon on getting *Troides goliath*.

That trip, however, has yet to be made. After the Solomons, I was tempted to explore Dutch New Guinea: but this year, or the next, I hope to get farther into the Papuan Hinterland from Giriwa River. I am convinced that there are some fine discoveries yet to be made in the inland valleys among the great mountains of British New Guinea.

CHAPTER XI

THE SOLOMONS AGAIN: I GROW WEARY OF THE SOUTH SEAS LIFE

I HAD been discussing for some time with the authorities of the Tring Museum the matter of a collecting trip in the Solomons which would comprise some inland exploration. In 1906 I wrote to them: "Regarding the inland Solomon Islands collections, I go there immediately on completion of this collection on the north-east coast of New Guinea. You previously arranged with me to take a mountain collection from both Ysabel and Guadalcanar Islands. I am sorry you 'have no faith in Guadalcanar.' Perhaps I can explain it. Where all the collecting has been done there, so far, has been on Aola on the north coast, where the country is very flat with the exception of a few crags and ridges close to the coast; but at either end of the island or anywhere along the southern coast the 'true' hills come down to the coast. Hence all the collecting has been done on comparatively young or 'made' country, not like the true formation. (I always notice on islands of basaltic or coral origin that the fauna is very scarce and comparatively nothing indigenous to the island occurs. This accounts for my want of faith in Rennel Island

and my strong faith in Santa Cruz.) If I made a mountain trip on Guadalcanar, as I had intended, I should go through the low-lying country and get into the 'true' mountains, where my experience always has been that collecting can be carried out under conditions very much more favourable for success than where the hills come down to the sea. (I mean when one is going for mountain species only and not to make a general all-round collection.) The reason I collected at Aola was partly owing to want of knowledge on my part and partly because the natives were at that time too bad elsewhere. I have every faith in Guadalcanar, if only for the fact of its being the only island in the Solomons where it is practicable to get to any height, with the exception of Bougainville. I am not quite mad enough to attempt a mountain trip there—at least not without knowing a great deal more than I know at present.

"*Re* the mountains of New Georgia. The hills on New Georgia (there are no mountains) are of a basaltic nature. The natives there dig out clam shells from the top of them, for making native money. They must be very recent hills. On Vangago and Gotakai there are fairly high mountains. I shall be collecting on either one of them. I shall also be collecting on Rossel Island, but I have no faith in doing much good there, it being of low coral formation. (I forgot, though: there is one fairly high hill or mountain on

New Georgia which has a pillar on it, and is used as a bearing on the charts.)

"*Re* Rennell Island. As I wrote you before, this will rest with yourselves. If I thought there was much to be got there, I should want no guarantee, but I am quite certain it would pay no man to go there and be paid by results."

Now there had come reports of a new butterfly having been discovered at Bougainville, and the Tring Museum was keen to get some specimens. The discovery had been made by one of the Roman Catholic Fathers of the Sacred Heart Mission, who was collecting for a friend in Luxembourg. The butterfly in question was a close relative of the *Papilio laglaizei*, only much darker. The quest of this particular butterfly was the chief object of this collecting trip to Bougainville, though not, of course, the only object.

I left Samarai on September 30, 1907, and reached Ronongo a week later, staying there three days whilst making some alterations to my ship's gear, and fitting to her another topmast. I reached Gizo on October 10. I had a fairly good trip across, with no very heavy weather, but big seas and constant heavy rain-squalls, accompanied by thunder and lightning. I was pleased when we got into sheltered waters and anchored, as I was rather anxious on account of the barometer falling very low—lower than it had done in the hurricane a month previously in New Guinea.

I went up on the north side of Bougainville, where the German Government had just established a Station. There was a German doctor at this station, who visited me on the *Shamrock*, and I was surprised to find him talking " pidgin " English to me. I found that it was the only English that he knew, and that he had found it necessary to learn it in order to talk with the natives, who understood something of " pidgin " English, but nothing of any other European language. Usually the European uses " pidgin " English to the natives, but never dreams of using it to another white man. However, my German friend, as I have said, talked " pidgin " English, and I rather welcomed it as a proof of the fact that the English language was more general than any other among the natives of that quarter. I paid my port dues to the German authorities, not being anxious, or even willing, to smuggle into German territory on this occasion; and then went cruising round the coast.

I made a camp on the north side of the island, and stayed there for a month, collecting. The results were pretty fair, but not very good. No notable new discovery was made, and I did not get specimens of the particular butterfly I was hunting after. On one or two occasions I made voyages from the coast up to the mountains, but saw nothing worth stopping for.

The natives of that district were singular from any other natives in the South Seas that I had encountered in having a wicker-work industry. They made large plaited bowls for use as food baskets. Their complexion was extremely dark. The placing together of the Solomon Islands in one group is purely arbitrary, for different islands are inhabited by widely different peoples. East of Choiseul Island the people are light; west of Choiseul they are very dark. I noticed that among the dark tribes you would often find a light specimen, owing to the fact that the dark tribes would sometimes raid the light tribes on head-hunting expeditions and bring back with them as slaves either women or young children. But among the light tribes you would never find specimens of the dark race, for the reason that the light tribes never raided in a westerly direction, but carried on their marauding farther east.

After staying about a month at this spot on the north side of Bougainville, I went to the south coast of the island, still in search of my particular butterfly. It took me in all three days to get to the Bougainville Straits, as the weather was very calm. In the straits I was becalmed for some hours. Then, of a sudden, a white squall came up. I had had just enough warning to take in the topsails when the storm was upon us, and in a moment sea and sky came together as our boat was sent scudding through the foam with her rail under water. I managed to get to the sheets and to lower the mizzen and stay sails. Then, with only the foresail, we rushed before the wind. I ran

DUBU, SOLOMON ISLANDS.

half-way around an island and then noticed a tiny break in the line of the reef indicated by a lane of unbroken water. It was not more than eighteen feet in width, this opening, and it gave entrance to a little cove which barely gave us room to swing around. But, small as was the haven, we were profoundly thankful for it, and we rode out the storm there in safety.

In this little retreat I stopped two days waiting for the wind to moderate. When at last I ventured out the wind was still strong, so strong that I noticed a swallow trying to fly against it and giving up the attempt finally, and then coming down the wind and striking the rigging of my boat, where it was killed.

Landing at a German Mission Station on the south side of the island, I rented a native house, or dubu, where the villagers kept their ceremonious drums. It was a kind of concert hall. The drums were stored in this house, and when a dance or other festivity was contemplated the natives assembled there. I found the natives of this quarter very kind and hospitable. Fortunately so for me, for I encountered here a very serious sickness. It was not the fever alone. The fever I had come to expect as part of the ordinary routine of island life. But in addition to the fever I had a very serious abscess on my left shoulder. It was due, I think, to the harsh living, and the poor food that was forced upon me by the character of my expeditions. I was laid up for a while and could not move. I attempted no medical treatment, except putting some ointment on the abscess. It got all right in time: most things do if you leave them alone long enough. It was not the first time that I had suffered from abscesses. Sometimes, after long spells of poor food without a sufficient supply of vegetables in tropical districts, my blood would get poor, and the sign of this would be the breaking out of painful abscesses.

Though I was ill and could not move most of the time, my boys, assisted by the local natives, did some collecting under my direction, and I got specimens of the butterfly that I wanted; not very many, but sufficient for my purpose. Apart from that I remember getting nothing new that was notable.

The last few years have made a great difference in the people of Bougainville, and there are now plenty of places on the coast where a person will be in perfect safety. But men are not able to go far into the interior yet, excepting as far as the flat land is concerned. The high ranges have not been explored so far.

I was able to collect nothing but what I had got on a previous trip to the Solomon Islands, excepting the *Papilio*, of which I obtained about forty bred specimens. I also collected three specimens of a *Papilio* which seemed vaguely familiar but which I could not place. It is a smaller edition of *codrus* in shape and colour, but with more colour, and the

THE SOLOMONS AGAIN

female has white in the hind-wings while the male has the same colour in both wings.[1] But as I have said I was unable to collect properly on the mountains, as the natives "backed out" of carrying, and as I was ill I had to work from the shore, my boys going up the mountains every day until they tired of getting nothing. The scrub was all second growth away from the fringe of the coast. There was no virgin forest so far as my boys penetrated, and, consequently, little hope of new discoveries.

I got no new birds additional to those I had obtained previously. The *Microgoura* I was satisfied does not occur on Bougainville, though I was told by native boys that it is found on both Ysabel and Malaita.[2]

Leaving Bougainville I sent away my collections and went down to Vella Levella, where I put my vessel up in a very small anchorage in a place that was infested with crocodiles. These crocodiles never molested me, and they came in handy when I wanted meat for my boys. I made a camp ashore near the beach and started collecting, getting very little that was new in lepidoptera, but it was a very picturesque place to stay. The coast line is broken into numberless tiny bays studded with little islands of great beauty. There are some thousands of islands, some

---

[1] *Papilio mendana acous* Ribbe (1898).—K. J.
[2] This extraordinary pigeon (*Microgoura meeki*) is fully described and figured in *Nov. Zool.*, 1904.

of them no larger than a room; and on an occasional island the natives have built temples in which are stored human skulls adorned with beads and feathers. These islands are treated as shrines.

Interesting souvenirs of a prehistoric life on the islands were the tablets made of petrified clam shells. These tablets were pierced with eye-holes, sometimes in two rows; and beneath these eye-holes were rows and rows of carved figures, and designs in scroll-work. The figures were of two or three different types repeated over and over again.

The natives of the present generation have no idea of carving in this way. Nor can they tell where these tablets came from, except that they are found in caves in the hills and that they "are made by the devil." The natives offered one day to show me a place "which the devil had made." It was unlike, they said, any other place in the world, and it was high up in the mountains. One day I took an expedition to this "Palace of Satan," and I came upon a very curious natural formation. There was a great precipice, with the face of it so tessellated by some natural agency that it looked as though it had been built up of masonry. Until I came to examine the cliff-wall closely, I had an idea that it was the work of some prehistoric masons.

The natives of this district, like most natives of New Guinea and the surrounding islands, are fond of attributing a great degree of activity to the devil.

Many things are put down to the devil, from the inconvenience of a fish-bone stuck in one's throat to a bad attack of fever. They have a much more vivid idea of the devil than of any Good Spirit. I cannot recollect, indeed, in the course of all my conversations with the natives, any direct reference to a Good Spirit, though allusions to the devil, to the magic that he might work, and to the necessity of conciliating him were very frequent.

After collecting at this spot in Vella Levella for a month, I cruised slowly along the coast, not setting up tents in the evenings but camping in my boat. One day I came across a solitary trader's house, and found him very sick with fever. The best I could do for him was to catch some fresh fish for him, with the agency, as usual, of a plug of dynamite. The poor fellow had a native wife in Ellis Island, whom he had left behind whilst he was on a trading trip to this quarter. He entrusted to me some "trade" that he wished to have sent to her. I heard shortly afterwards of his death.

The white traders in the South Sea Islands often contract marriages with native women, and in many cases these marriages, ill-fitting though they may seem, endure for quite a long time, especially when any family grows up as a result of the union. Of course, a native woman of any intelligence who has lived as his wife with a trader for some length of time comes to be very useful to him in his business;

and that becomes a bond, helping to stability of the tie.

I went back to Gizo to send forward my collections to Europe, and there the man who was looking after the *Shamrock* for me confessed himself sick of the life of the islands, and asked leave to go back to New Guinea. He had some £40 or £50 due to him for wages, and I advanced him some more money and helped him to buy a small cutter in which he embarked for New Guinea. He had rather a bad passage and was obliged to land at Sudest Island to replenish his supply of water. Whilst he was ashore there the *Merrie Englande* put in to the island and placed his boat under arrest because he had committed an offence in landing at Sudest without having clearance papers from any port. Under the circumstances, however, no trouble was made for him. I merely refer to the incident to show how closely the Australian Government patrols the coast of its possessions in the South Seas.

On board the *Merrie Englande* at the time was Miss Beatrice Grimshaw, who has written much about the South Seas. My sailor man told me afterwards that the meeting was an amusing one. He heard her remark to the captain of the *Merrie Englande:* " Did he come all the way from the Solomons in that little boat ? "

" Yes," was the reply.

" Then he must be mad," the lady said emphatically.

According to his own account my sailor man then broke in, lifting his hat and saying, "Yes, lady. If I were not mad I would not be here."

From Vella Levella I made my way to the extreme east of the Solomon Islands, beating up against the wind to St. Christabel, and putting in at Guadalcanar on the way. I found some English planters there who had built a very nice house for their comfort, fitted up, if you please, with billiard room and a billiard table. I reflected that life in the South Seas was losing its savage charm when these evidences of civilisation began to appear. Nevertheless I enjoyed very much the hospitality of the planters.

Farther on, in a very small bay on one side of Guadalcanar Island, I encountered a white man who was trading in copra for a Sydney firm. He had not seen a white man for six months and was very pleased to see me. He was singularly amiable and gentle when sober, but entirely different when drunk. I am afraid it is a fact that many traders in the South Seas are tempted by the lonely life to drunkenness, gin being the favourite drink. Gin, or something of the sort, accounts for most of the cases of cruelty that now and again occur on the islands.

I do not wish to be misunderstood in this reference to "cruelty." I have no sympathy with the sentimental rubbish that is talked in some quarters in regard to the treatment of natives. In my experience one must be firm with them and sometimes it is necessary to inflict punishment when they attempt any nonsense. In effect, I find that you must treat the natives like you would treat the boys of a junior school, a school from which the cane has not been abolished. But any acts of cruelty, that is to say, of causeless infliction of pain, do no good at all to white interests in the Pacific, apart from the unhappiness they inflict on the natives. In my opinion if a white man in those quarters is convicted more than once of cruelty to the natives he should be prevented for ever after from having native men under him.

It is an unfortunate thing that for the acts of cruelty of some white man in the Islands other white men, quite innocent of such acts, may have to suffer. When deeds of cruelty are inflicted the natives get into their heads a hatred, not so much of the man who has done the cruel deed, as of all white men; and a quite guiltless trader may suffer with his life for the drunken or careless cruelty of another many miles away.

I found San Christoval Island a very poor place for collecting, it being all limestone country and not at all rich either in vegetation or in lepidoptera. Nearly all the male natives of this island have been away at some time or another on white plantations, either in Queensland or elsewhere, and so they were all fairly civilised, spoke good English and were very entertaining when talking over their experiences of civilisation. A less happy sign of their having come into close contact with white life was the prevalence of consumption and of a still more dreadful disease.

Coming away from San Christoval I encountered a great storm, with rain and almost continuous lightning. It was at the time of the change from the N.W. to the S.E. monsoons. I ran before the storm under bare poles for some hours, and when the wind moderated a little I set the mizzen and the jib and hove to. It was the wildest night at sea in my experience.

I got to the little bay where the white traders of the luxurious life were and rested there gratefully a whole day. From the natives of the bay I got on this occasion some of their spears, which are made of the shin bones of men, which are carved into very fine lace work. From there I went along the coast to Ysabel Island, not doing much collecting, but buying turtle shells and native money; and then made my way to Gizo.

To bear out what I have just said about native outrages; I was on this occasion just outside Marabou lagoon when the trader who some time previously had bought the *Hekla* from me was being killed by the natives. He was sitting on the rail of his little vessel when the natives came in a canoe and tomahawked him from behind his back. His name was Oliver, and so far as I know he had never done anything himself to incur the resentment of the natives. But just at that time a native boy who had been shut up in Gizo gaol for some offence had hanged himself in prison, and the natives, probably having a garbled version of the incident, were very angry against all white men for that particular reason. I heard of the tragedy at Gizo and thought that the fate of Oliver might very well have been mine if it had happened that I had been camping inside the lagoon and not keeping a good watch.

The boy in gaol had no reason of cruelty to explain his suicide. Gaol life in those parts of Oceania which are under British rule is quite free from all harshness. Here is an official report of the routine of Port Moresby gaol—the chief gaol in Papua:

" Cell doors are opened at 5.30 a.m. Blankets aired, rolled up, and put away on shelf on verandah built for that purpose, so leaving all cells empty during the day time. The cells are swept clean by the female prisoners after breakfast every morning. Breakfast is served at 6.15 a.m. At 6.45 a.m. all prisoners are lined up, drilled and the roll called. The different gangs with their warders are then despatched to their respective duties. At noon the mid-day meal is served at the most convenient locality to which they may be working. Work is resumed at 1 p.m., which is continued until 5 p.m. Supper is served at 5.20 p.m., and at 6 p.m. all are lined up, roll called, dismissed to their cells and locked up for the night with the exception of those absolutely necessary for maintenance of gaol discipline. All work is sus-

PRISON AND PRISONERS, SAMARAI.

pended every Saturday at noon where practicable. Saturday afternoon is devoted to washing clothes. Every native prisoner must appear in clean clothes before he receives his weekly allowance of tobacco, which is served out every Saturday afternoon. The prisoners are employed at excavations for Government buildings, discharging and handling cargo, and coaling the *Merrie Englande*. The roads and streets at and around Port Moresby are kept clean. All sanitary works are carefully attended to by prison labour; a gang of twelve prisoners and two prison warders are constantly employed at this work. All public buildings are painted, lime-washed; house piles and fencing posts are tarred when necessary; also fencing and all other rough repairs are done by prison labour. A gang is always kept road-making when available."

A term in gaol is often indeed the beginning of a new life for the native, in which he adopts some of the ways of civilisation that he has learned whilst under arrest.

From Gizo I went on to Samarai, very much out of conceit with the island life, my ideas of it being strongly coloured for a time by the thought of the tragedy. From Samarai I made a run to Buna Bay, which I reached about June 14, 1908. After discharging cargo, I got carriers and went inland to where I had got the *Troides alexandrae* previously. I did not succeed in getting many specimens but got a lot of fever and sickness instead. I had erysipelas of the knee and leg and was laid up for a week. On the first day I was able to walk, I went down to Buna Bay in teeming rain. Next day two lumps started in the knee and inside the lower thigh. It was about a fortnight before they burst, and then only when I had cut them with a razor. They seemed to start somewhere deep inside the leg and the whole limb swelled up until the inflammatory matter found an outlet. I never in my life suffered such excruciating agony as I did this time coming down to the coast; and this illness pulled me down to a thinner state than I had been in for thirteen years, since I first went to the South Seas. Fortunately I got to Samarai in safety, but a good deal wearied with the South Sea island life and very clearly resolved on a long holiday in Australia to recruit my shattered health. I found awaiting me letters from the Tring Museum urging upon me an expedition to Rennell Island. It was quite the most unfavourable time to get such a request. I was more inclined to give up collecting altogether than to undertake a trip which would have been the most dangerous I had yet attempted. Accordingly I wrote back to the Museum authorities:

"I am quite willing to visit Rennell Island but expect to be remunerated for doing so, whether successful in collecting or not. To go to such a place, that has no anchorage, with a big chance of losing one's life either by sea or on land, is rather a steep

PRISONERS AT WORK, SAMARAI.

To face p. 196.

THE SOLOMONS AGAIN

venture. If I go there I want to do some satisfactory work, and if I undertake to go no trifle will stop me from work. But I do not relish going. Still, as I said before, it rests entirely with yourselves and Mr. Rothschild. If the cost of the expedition (some £400) is guaranteed the expedition will be made. I do not want you to think I am exaggerating. I think I know just about as much about the dangers as any one else, and I am not afraid of danger. Still, I am not keen on Rennell Island. Any person who is not absolutely an idiot could visit there with a guard of a dozen police with rifles, but to work there for a long spell is a different matter altogether. I have only heard of two men who ever landed there. One had some difficulty in getting off the beach because he paid the natives (or tried to) in tobacco for some native food he had got. They tried to seize him and his boat's crew because they did not understand tobacco's use. The other was a Roturnah man, who shot one of the Rennell Islanders because they were trying to take away his firearms. Still, I am willing to go *anywhere* provided there is the glimmer of a chance of getting out again ! If I visit Rennell Island it would be after the Solomon Islands are finished, so that if anything did happen to me you would have the Solomon collections completed."

I think this must have convinced the Tring Museum authorities that the island in question was really impracticable, for nothing more was said about an expedition there.

I do not know whether the tragedy of the *Hekla* had affected my nerves in any way, but I really intended to abandon the South Seas for a while at this time. From Samarai I crossed to Queensland, bidding farewell to the wild life of the South Seas. I had done that before, half seriously, but on this occasion I genuinely thought that I meant to settle down in Queensland. I accepted an invitation to go to the Barnards' Station, where I was received with very much kindness and amused myself for some months shooting kangaroos.

CHAPTER XII

AT THE FOOT OF THE SNOW MOUNTAINS

KANGAROO shooting I found to have sufficient of adventure and excitement to keep my thoughts off butterfly expeditions for nearly six months. Then I began to be weary of what seemed to me an objectless sort of life. I think that after a while the wish for travelling gets into the blood and becomes a disease. I know that I am now always intolerant of staying in any one place for more than a few months. Sometimes in New Guinea, sick of the fever, appalled at the loneliness of my position many days away from any white friends, I have decided to leave New Guinea for ever and have upbraided myself as a fool for undertaking the hardships of such a life. Then, having got away from New Guinea and reached a life of civilisation in Australia, after a little while I have found the charm of the jungle and the excitement of life as a collector pull me back.

I was beginning, as I have said, to feel a weariness of life without dangers and without any serious purpose when a letter from Tring sent my thoughts back to collecting. In my correspondence with the Tring Museum the undertaking of an expedition to the Charles Louis Mountains in Dutch New Guinea had been mentioned for years, now and again, but I had hitherto been very reluctant to enter upon such an expedition as I was afraid of the cost. Now this project was revived and I answered promptly (Sept. 4, 1909):

"I shall be only too happy to start whenever you please; I am tired of doing nothing, just as much tired as I sometimes get of being in New Guinea. I expect I shall end my days there. I was considering the advisability of attempting something over there when your letter came. No one who ever lives a great while in the South Sea Islands but is sure to return there sooner or later. The islands always seem to be calling, and to make one dissatisfied elsewhere. If you care I could make a start early in April to recruit boys, and could get up to Dutch New Guinea somewhere about July."

When preparing for this expedition I heard that the British Ornithologists' Union was also organising an expedition to Dutch New Guinea. However, the news did not disturb me much in completing my preparations. There was plenty of room for many expeditions in the enormous mountain range I intended to reach, and the only serious drawback of another party having been in the place was this, that the natives might possibly be spoiled by them in one way or the other.

I left Sydney in February of 1910 for Samarai by way of the Solomons for this my last big expedition to date. At Samarai I picked up my boat the *Shamrock*, and completed the outfitting which I had begun at Sydney. This was to be a very big expedition, and my preparations were on a far larger scale than they ever had been before. At Samarai I was fortunate enough to be able to have transferred to me twelve native boys who had been engaged for work on the goldfields. I had to pay £65 to the recruiting agent for the transfer.

I left on May 1st for Port Moresby, and after a voyage of four days' length took my clearance out for Dutch New Guinea by way of Thursday Island. The route I took to Thursday Island took us past Yule Island and the famous Bramble Cay sandbank. As we neared Bramble Cay I noticed the sea-birds hovering over it like a cloud, or like the column of smoke that goes up from a bush fire starting on the horizon. Curiosity made me anchor my boat near by so that I might visit the sandbank.

With a boat's crew of native boys we pulled to Bramble Cay. The noise made by the birds as we disturbed them was shrill and almost deafening. To say that the birds were there in millions, and many millions at that, is not at all an exaggeration. They were mostly terns, black and white, and they had come to the "island" to lay and hatch out their eggs. The "island" is little more than a great sandbank, very low in the water, covered with coarse herbage growing to a height of a few inches. In this herbage the nests were so thick that it was almost impossible to walk along the sands without treading upon eggs. Fortunately most of the eggs were fresh.

We took away from Bramble Cay a large stock of eggs, much to the delight of my native boys, whose eyes fairly goggled with excitement as they saw the number of birds and of birds' eggs. They took off their loin clothes to make bags for holding the eggs.

Another source of wild delight to the boys was to see the great number of clam shells on the edge of the shore. On the coast of Papua the population is so thick that the clams have almost been eaten out, and in some cases the natives have to dive for them. The fishing grounds also have been thinned out very seriously. This is so much the case that the different tribes on the coast of New Guinea now have their fishing grounds sharply defined, and poaching and trespassing off your own ground is strictly forbidden.

Those of my boys who had come from the New Guinea coast had never seen before in their lives so much tucker as they did on their way to Thursday Island. It was not only that they had the great supply of sea-birds' eggs at Bramble Cay, but at all the little islands which we encountered there were huge supplies of fish. I recollect once noticing my cook, a native boy who was a very clever little chap, lying on his belly in front of a little pool near the shore. "Me get one small fish!" he said with a grin as I stood over him, and pulled out a huge rock

AT FOOT OF THE SNOW MOUNTAINS 203

cod, bit its neck so as to kill it, and put it by his side on the reef. He then plunged his arm in for another and got two fine fish out of the one small pool. That was wonderful fishing from his point of view.

Every day on our way to Thursday Island we anchored at some little island. It would have perhaps suited me better in one way to have pushed on, sailing both day and night; but I got a great deal of fun out of the enjoyment of my boys at these intermediate islands, and the generous feeding put them in good heart for the hardships that were to follow. Besides, in the South Seas there is none of the wild rush of a civilised city. There are no trains to catch, no newspapers to bring out, nothing to be done that must be done now. It is a land of lots of time.

Entering Thursday Island harbour I found all the flags on the shipping flying at half-mast, and learnt that this was in consequence of King Edward's death. Of course I half-masted our vessel's flag and explained to the boys why this mark of respect was shown. It fell to me to convey the news of the death of King Edward to Dutch New Guinea when I arrived there.

At Thursday Island I completed the taking in of my supply of provisions, shipping the stores that had come up from Sydney—mostly tinned foods, fish, meat, and groceries. (At Samarai I had taken in three tons of rice.) I found awaiting me at Thursday Island letters of introduction from Burns Philp & Co., to the Dutch authorities at Merauke.

Sailing from Thursday Island I took a North-West course and encountered a sandbank called Tara Cay, which was not marked on my chart, but which I found later is marked on up-to-date charts. The place I found to be one great nest for turtles. Their nests were strewn all around in the sand, some of them old ones, some of them recent and containing fresh eggs. My cook boy proved very clever at distinguishing the recent ones. The usual method of exploring was to take a long sharp stick and poke it into the ground where it seemed to be disturbed. If you struck eggs your stick showed the mark of them; and you had also a rough indication as to whether the eggs were fresh or not. My native cook seemed to be able to know by instinct where there was a nest with fresh eggs.

The hunting skill of savage races—enabling them to obtain food with the help of very primitive weapons—strikes the civilised observer as being little short of the miraculous. The Australian aboriginal is supposed to be a very low type of savage. But he has almost superhuman intelligence when he is faced with the problem of the chase. His hunting is not a mere matter of endurance, speed or accuracy of aim with his poor weapons; it is intelligent observation brought to a fine art. The blackfellow knows the track, cry and habits of every animal, and takes advantage of its peculiarity or characteristic to secure its downfall. This knowledge of animals is linked to

AT FOOT OF THE SNOW MOUNTAINS

inexhaustible patience and perseverance. He will track the 'possum by its claw-marks on a tree-trunk, or by observing the flight of mosquitoes if no claw-marks are visible. He will decoy pelicans within his reach by imitating the disturbance of water from the jumping of fish by throwing mussel-shells into a pond or splashing it with his fingers. He will creep or swim up to ducks with grass round his head and pull the birds one by one under water, breaking their necks and letting them float till he has enough for his needs. He will find and capture snakes by watching the movements of their companions, the butcher birds. He will catch a bee, stick a piece of feather or down on it, let it go, and follow its flight until he finds its hive and honey. He will walk into the sea at a place where a white man cannot see a single shell and in a few minutes, by digging in the spots of yielding sand with his feet, find enough cockles for his meal. He can find food where a white man would starve to death.

This ingenuity is seen almost as much in fishing as in hunting. Hooks made of shells or tortoise-shell, harpoons, spears, baskets, cages, nets, hollow log traps, weirs, dams, fences and poisoning are all employed as a means of obtaining fish. He will, indeed, use one fish to catch another. The remora or sucker-fish, with a string attached to its tail, is used to help the blackfellow to turtle, dugong, or to other food-fish.

The huge beds of cockle-shells, some of them about a mile long and hundreds of yards across, with ovens of flat stones, found among the sandhills near the shore, in parts of Australia, show the enormous numbers of molluscs the aboriginal gathered and cooked. The big inland fishing weirs offer further evidence of his ingenuity as a fisherman.

And the Australian aboriginal is an expert water-finder. By looking at certain vegetation or noting the fall of the ground, he is able to tell where and at what depth water will be found, and he sinks his water-hole accordingly. He knows where he will find water after a shower or on a dewy morning, which he can collect and store in his water bag. One tribe, which lived where water was at times very scarce, learned to seal up the sutures of skulls, which were then used for water-carrying. It is known to the white travellers in Australia that in any kind of country, however desert and waterless it seems, the natives can lead them to stores of water. There have been some grim incidents because of natives either misunderstanding or wilfully disobeying the orders of white travellers in the desert to lead them to water. Stupidity or disobedience has been met with torture. In one case, which caused a painful sensation when the facts became known, some white travellers, perishing with thirst, flogged two natives to make them disclose the locality of their wells and, that failing, filled the mouths of the blackfellows with

AT FOOT OF THE SNOW MOUNTAINS 207

salt and exposed them, bound and gagged, to the full heat of the sun until they led the way to water.

But let us get back to the more pleasant proof of the savage skill in hunting, afforded by my cook boy, who seemed to be able to tell a turtle nest with fresh eggs from a nest with stale eggs by the mere appearance of the sand. The turtle egg of course has no hard shell. It is soft and round, something the shape of an india-rubber ball with a dent in it. We collected a great number of the eggs for food for the boys and decided to pay a visit to the sandbank by night, in the hope of thus getting some fresh turtle. The sandbank was about half a mile long and obviously it had been sometimes visited by pearl-divers' crews, or by some other human beings, for the turtles did not stay ashore near their nests, but only visited the place on the top of the tide. In other places, where they are not disturbed, you will find the turtles basking about on the sandbanks near their nests in the laying season.

Going ashore in the dark we encountered a great deal of difficulty on account of the fast running of the tide, but we succeeded in getting safely to the bank and captured a couple of turtles weighing about 3 cwt. each—the big, green-fat, eating turtles. One we took away to our vessel that night in the dinghy and left the other (turned upon its back so that it could not escape), and collected it in the morning.

These large turtles have very strong jaws and their bite can be very dangerous. I have seen one crush a great branch of coral in its teeth. They seem to have very little brains, however, and I do not think they attempt to defend themselves. If you encounter a bite from one it is by way of accident. The flesh of roast turtle is very like beef. I do not care to eat the green fat which is prized so much by some as a delicacy for soup.

From Tara Cay, making an early start we ran along until three o'clock the next morning, when by log reckoning I calculated that we must be near Merauke, and so I hove to. My calculations proved to be correct, for the next morning at dawn we picked up the land, which is very low-lying. The first thing I saw was a grass fire which had been made by the natives for the purpose of hunting game. The chart I had, as I had discovered before at Tara Cay, was an old-fashioned one, and I could not quite identify the indications for the Port of Merauke. But I noticed a small boat going up a river and followed it in. It was Sunday, and everybody seemed to be making holiday and no one took any particular notice of our arrival. I understood that I should have to get *pratique* from the Port doctor, so I ran up a blue flag, which was the flag asking for a doctor in my signal book. That, like the chart, however, was out of date. I should have run up a yellow flag.

There came no reply to my blue flag, so I went ashore and encountered a Eurasian official who was puzzling over the blue flag, and referring to his signal

AT FOOT OF THE SNOW MOUNTAINS

book. I had no Malay or Dutch and he had no English; but he was a civil and obliging official and granted me *pratique* on general principles, and I made my way to the house of a trader name Mr. Smoos, who could speak English, as indeed most of the Dutch residents of the town could. It seemed that the Governor-General of the Dutch Indies had written to the officials of Dutch New Guinea asking them to do what they could to help me in my expedition, and all the officials proved very kind and hospitable. I was at once introduced to a little club that the Dutch residents had in the town and which was called "the kia-kia club." Kia-kia is the native word for peace in that locality, and the Dutch called the natives kia-kias because, on encountering a white man, they would usually make that their first cry.

With very great kindness the Dutch resident, Mr. Hellwig, informed me that the Dutch Government were just then organising two expeditions, one of which had for its objective the Snow Mountains and the other the sources of the Island River, and he told me that I had permission to use the Government steamers and Government launches, which were engaged for those expeditions, to help me along my course. Their work of course was purely exploring.

Very grateful for this kindness, I spent a happy fortnight in Merauke dismantling my ship, putting the final touches to my outfit and occasionally taking short shooting expeditions to get some crocodiles and wallaby for my boys to eat. The stay in Merauke was necessary because the Government steamer had not returned. I reported to Tring Museum from Merauke (May 28, 1910):

"I arrived here some six days ago from Thursday Island, and awaited here the arrival of the Assistant-Resident and the Controller, who were both away on expeditions. They both arrived here some two days ago. The Assistant-Resident, who is the chief in rank, had received instructions from the Governor-General of the Dutch Indies to assist me all he could when I arrived. This was due to Burns, Philp & Co. (who are now running large steamers to Java and other Dutch islands besides opening branches), writing to the Dutch Consul-General in Melbourne for the letters for me. I had other letters from local Consuls in Sydney, Brisbane, and Thursday Island. It is in consequence of this that I am to be allowed to join the military expedition up the Oetakwa River, under the Snowy Mountains. Whether I shall be able to get high enough is a question I shall be able to reply to later. I leave the *Shamrock* moored here and join the *Valk* (the Government exploring steamer) on the 9th to the Oetakwa River, then go in the *Saunek* for five hours. Then there is a two days' journey in canoes, and thence overland. The natives there are not very peaceable, and it would not be possible to work there excepting with a large Government force close at hand to keep the peace.

DUTCH EXPLORERS' CAMP, OETAKWA RIVER.

AT FOOT OF THE SNOW MOUNTAINS

"The Goodfellow Expedition is at the Mimika. The captain of the *Valk* told me that Dr. E. Marshal died there lately, this being the second death of a white member of the party. Until lately they had no boys for transport, and some of the members have been in Fak Fak, while Mr. Goodfellow went to Manaosu trying to get coolies. He has just returned with sixty from Ambou, but only under two months' agreement. The Dutch Government have loaned him two lifeboats and a steam launch, and have also given him forty (40) soldiers, three sergeants and a white officer. The people here do not think he will reach the Snow Mountains. If so it will be a very great pity, after all the trouble and expense that he has incurred."

I left Merauke on the Dutch patrol boat and we made our way along the coast to the Oetakwa River, some 300 miles in a north-westerly direction, passing through the Marianne Straits between Prince Frederick Henry Island and the mainland. Off the Oetakwa River we had a very beautiful view of the Snow Mountains in the distance, with the white-covered peaks broken here and there by great patches of black rock.

At the mouth of the Oetakwa River we disembarked our baggage into launches. The stores for the Dutch expedition filled nine big boats and my stores another big boat. This string of boats was taken into tow by a steam launch, and like a great snake it wound its way up the river, a full day's journey. This was the end of navigable water for the steam launch. At this stage, which was called the Launch Stage, I encountered Captain Van der Bie and discussed my arrangements with him. Then two days' journey further up the river by canoe brought us to what was called the Canoe Stage. I was allowed the use of one canoe to get my things up. At first I was allowed also the help of a couple of Malays who understood the ways of the river, and of the canoes. With their help on the first trip we got along all right. Afterwards my boys were left to themselves, and as they were not used to the work, either to shooting rapids downstream or towing the canoe through them up against the stream, we had a fairly exciting time. On the last trip up when the canoe was actually in sight of Canoe Camp we had an accident. In negotiating a rapid, the canoe struck a stone which broke her almost in half.

We lost a great deal of stores. All the biscuits, salt, raincoats, mosquito nets, blankets, four mats of rice, three pairs of boots, and other things were washed away. I was rather badly bruised on the stones and my feet cut about, as I had been rolled almost the length of the rapid after losing my footing. Eventually some of the things were rescued and nothing of the first importance was found to be lost. The canoe was lent me by the Military Exploration party, and now I had to depend on them to assist me in getting up the remainder of my rice for the boys. I had left twenty-seven mats of rice in the jungle fifteen days before.

CANOE CAMP, OETAKWA RIVER.

AT FOOT OF THE SNOW MOUNTAINS

The Canoe Camp was situated on the right-hand branch of the Oetakwa. The journey to it was about three hours by steamer, then eighteen hours by launch, and then a day and half by canoe journey. The last stage of the river is nothing but a succession of rapids, which generally are negotiated by aid of a tow-rope.

I bought two canoes at the mouth of the river from the natives, but found them absolutely impracticable in the rapids and left them behind. I had to depend entirely then on the Bornean canoes belonging to the Dutch Military Expedition.

When I got to Canoe Camp I found that the Dutch expedition was only a day or two ahead, and as the country looked fairly promising for lepidoptera I thought it best to start collecting, and so put up a grass house and made a camp there. It was impossible to enlist any help from the natives of the district. They were wild and nomadic in their habits, very timid and very dishonest. One saw them but seldom, and when they came to the camp it was usually in big numbers with the idea of thieving. They were of fine stature and wore little dress. Some of them indeed were stark naked. Their chief weapon was the bow and arrow and they had no spears, but used a kind of lance which was headed by the sharpened thigh-bone of the cassowary.

At this camp my first discovery of any note was a new sub-species of a Bird of Paradise. It is very closely allied to another species called *Parotia carolae*.

In fact without having the two together for comparison no one could detect the difference. I thought that the discovery was more important than it was, and sent the specimen home by post, writing to Dr. Hartert: " I send a pair of what I take to be a new Bird of Paradise. The male is unfortunately not fully plumaged; the belly showing as yet only young males' plumage. It is a *Parotia*, and the six plumes from the side of the head are very small, only about a third the size of those in *lawesi* and *helenae*. The crest is gold and chocolate in colour as in *helenae*, but the end over the beak is tipped with white. The crest, too, goes much further back, covering more than half the crown. It also has chocolate colour around the eyes. The female is much lighter in colour than is ordinary, and has the feathers of the crown of the head much closer and has also a smaller edition of a crest similar to that of the male."

I heard afterwards that the scientists at Tring Museum felt that they took some risk in describing this bird at all, for it was possible that the slight differences which it showed from the known species which it resembled were due to its lack of maturity. Afterwards, however, I got an adult male of this sub-species, which proved that it was entitled to the classification which had been ventured.[1]

[1] Mr. Rothschild described this bird under the name of *Parotia carolae meeki*, in honour of its discoverer. Although so very closely allied to the true *carolae*, it is to us of considerable interest from a zoogeographical point of view.—E. H.

AT FOOT OF THE SNOW MOUNTAINS 215

At this collecting station I got some other new birds of lesser importance, but the butterflies were disappointing. I therefore turned my thoughts towards the Snow Mountains. We could see them from my camp, looking very beautiful on a clear morning. We were only about thirty miles or so from them, but the country intervening seemed frightfully rough. Among the mountains was one peak of 12,000 feet. The snow fields near the summit of this appeared to be very extensive. Having sent a small collection away, I decided to make tracks for the mountains, not following the path which the Dutch had taken, but taking a route of my own. By so doing I avoided the risk of finding that collecting work had been spoiled by the dispersal of the birds and insects. Of course it does not necessarily follow that the passing of a few white men through a district will effect any very serious disturbance from a zoological point of view. But the chances are that with a large party breaking up the jungle, making fires, etc., there will be at least some disturbance of the insect and bird life. I prefer, therefore, when it is possible, to fix my collecting stations at places where no other white man has been.

On the way up from Canoe Camp, my own boys had to do all the carrying, because it was impossible to enlist any help from the natives. The country through which we passed was of a limestone formation, very savage and inhospitable. The limestone came out in sharp ridges and was also full of holes and caverns, making the march slow, difficult and painful. As a result of three days' hard work we got to a height of some 2500 feet, still in very inhospitable country, and still among timid and semi-hostile natives. The weather was hot and fever very bad in our camp. We found it impossible to get any native food, and so we had to do without vegetables. The only relief we had from the tinned food and rice which we carried with us was an occasional grilled pigeon.

I had set up two camps, one camp at two days' march from the Canoe Station, and a second camp at three days' march. The hardships of life were relieved by the fact that I was able to make very fine collections of moths by night. It is no exaggeration to say that I obtained scores of new species of moths, among them some new hawk moths, which are so-called on account of their very narrow, sharp, hard wings. I was also able to obtain some new birds, and finding the collecting so good I stayed from June to December, working harder than I had ever done before in New Guinea. The expedition had cost me at least £1200, and I was anxious to get as much return as possible for this large cost.

In December I had had a very cordial invitation from the Captain commanding the Island River Dutch Expedition, to join his forces. I also received a promise of the assistance of thirty carriers for one trip to carry up my gear to an altitude of five to six thousand feet, to a point from which a height of 10,000 feet would be available within three days' further journey. This offer I decided to avail myself of, and left for the coast on December 16, 1910, with the intention of collecting in Central Dutch New Guinea. The voyage, I learned, was by steamer up Island River 200 kilometres, by launch (two days), 80 kilometres, and by canoe (four days), 60 kilometres, then by road eight days' journey. Going by canoe there were to be a hundred and ten rapids to negotiate.

" Properly speaking," I wrote to the Tring Museum at the time, " I should not make this second collection, for my health has been such that only during last week has my right leg resumed its normal size. Previous to this I could press my finger into the leg anywhere and leave a deep hole of half an inch or so. These are all the symptoms of beri-beri (which it is not, for I have had it before). I have had one boy down with beri-beri at Oetakwa, but he pulled through."

There was no affectation in what I wrote to the Museum about the ill-advisedness, from a point of view of health, of undertaking a second collecting trip without a spell. The Oetakwa expedition had been a very trying one, partly on account of the impossibility of getting decent food, partly on account of the nervous strain of living constantly on guard against attack. Still the chance of getting to Central Dutch New Guinea was too good to be missed. I decided to make the venture, promising myself afterwards a long spell and a trip Home.

DUTCH OFFICERS' QUARTERS, ISLAND RIVER.

DUTCH EXPLORERS' CAMP, ISLAND RIVER.

CHAPTER XIII

IN CENTRAL DUTCH NEW GUINEA

It was in December 1910 that I learnt that the Dutch expedition to the Snow Mountains had found the difficulties of penetrating the inland country too great, and that they had received instructions from Captain Schafer, who was in general charge of both Dutch expeditions, to give up the attempt and descend the river. I received at the same time a very kind invitation from the Dutch authorities to join the Island River expedition, which was proving more successful. I therefore made my way down to Merauke, sent my collections forward to Europe, and joined the Island River party.

The Island River is a very fine stream which, on nearing the Dutch New Guinea coast, splits its great volume into branches, forming an extensive delta. It is possible to travel up the river by steamer 150 miles inland. When we had got that far by steamer we disembarked on to a hulk which had been moored there as a supply base for the expedition. At this hulk we repacked our stores and went up by steam launch a further two-days' journey. Then from this Launch Camp we were carried by canoes for four days up the stream of the river. The rapid character of the stream at this stage can be best judged from the fact that over 100 rapids are encountered during the four-days' journey, and that a distance which needs four days' hard travelling on the ascent can be covered within six hours in descending. The officers of the Dutch expedition were very hospitable to me, especially a naval officer, Captain Van der Van.

At the Canoe Camp, which marked the head of the navigable river, I started up towards the mountains again, using my own boys as carriers, as it was impossible to enlist any help from the natives around, who were very timid and not at all friendly. We journeyed four days into the interior, every day marking a great increase in elevation, for there were no foot-hills to be traversed. Finally I fixed a camp at the height of 6500 feet, or thereabouts, and sent the greater number of my boys back for more stores. Then I got the others to make a large clearing in the bush. Partly the purpose of this was to serve to attract moths at night; partly it was to make a more comfortable camping place for ourselves. The climate in this hill district is dank and miserable. When it is not raining one is liable to be soaked through and through by the great bodies of mist which come down from the mountain tops. The trees and shrubs drip constantly with wet. Insect life is abundant. It would thus have been impossible to have camped in any comfort without clearing away the forest and the undergrowth. I did not know that the clearing would have been resented so strongly by the natives of the district as it was; but had I known I would still have had to take the risk.

Life was there particularly miserable. At night the cold was intense, a damp, moist cold like that during the worst of a London fog. By day the weather was, when not cold and damp, humid. Never was there a clear, bright air. The forest trees, festooned with mosses which hung from the branches down to the very ground; the soil, covered with lichens which gave a foothold such as a soaking-wet sponge would—these gave always an impression of damp unwholesomeness. It was rare to be dry. The earth was wet, the trees wet, the atmosphere dripping always. To add to our hardships the food-supply was necessarily poor. It was impossible to obtain any provisions locally. All that we ate had to be carried a four-days' march from the Canoe Camp.

On the other hand, the collecting was simply glorious. The very first bird I shot was a new species of Bird of Paradise.[1] I collected there also specimens of the most beautiful Bird of Paradise that I know, the *Astrapia splendidissima*. I thought that this was a new discovery, and was much disappointed when I found out subsequently that Mr. Rothschild had described it fifteen years previously. I was

[1] The new Bird of Paradise mentioned by Mr. Meek is the very interesting *Paradigalla brevicauda*, described by Mr. Rothschild and myself; a coloured plate is published in the *Ibis* for 1912.—E. H.

further made happy by discovering ten or twelve new butterflies of the genus *Delias*. They are white butterflies as regards the top side of the wings, but on the under side the wings show the most beautiful colours: in some instances black and grey, in others black and red—all very peculiar and very beautiful. The males and the females of this genus are in some instances very much alike, except that the females are darker in colouring than the males.[1]

It needed such good collecting to atone for the hardships of the life there. The country had never been visited before by white people, and that, of course, made possible a number of new discoveries, but it also made it impossible to get on terms with the natives; so we were unable to secure any native food, and had to live on the tinned stores which we carried up from the coast. It would have been possible, of course—if I had chosen to sanction the attempt—to have raided some of the native villages near by for food; but during the course of my experiences as a collector I have never attempted any violent robbery. Occasionally a few pigeons which fell to our guns helped

[1] Besides these and other wonderful Birds of Paradise (among them the smallest of all *Paradiseidae*, *Loboparadisea sericea*, Rothsch., a new form of *Falcinellus striatus*, a young male of the most curious of all Birds of Paradise, the *Pteridophora alberti*), Mr. Meek discovered several new small birds; among them were three Honey-eaters, viz. *Melirrhophetes belfordi griseirostris*, *Ptilotis praeripna nigritergum* and *Melipotes gymnops goliathi*. The collection will be fully discussed in our journal, *Nov. Zool.*—E. H.

MY CAMP UNDER THE SNOW MOUNTAINS, DUTCH NEW GUINEA.

out our food-supply, but on the whole our dinners were detestable and our breakfasts and suppers likewise. So hard put were we for food that when a cassowary that I thought to be new fell to my gun, hunger was stronger than scientific curiosity and we promptly ate him without much thought of his value as a specimen.

I had cleared about three acres of land for our camp. Near its site was a large native village which, from what I could see, did not differ greatly from the hill villages in British New Guinea. But the natives made no friendly advances. Early one morning, however, when I was working in my tent I heard talking which I recognised was not that of my boys. I went out of the tent and found that a number of the natives from the village near by were gathered on a ridge some hundred yards away in a very excited state. They all had their weapons, and I gathered from their talk and from their gestures that they wanted to know why we were there, and why we had cut down trees. Also they made it very plain by signs that they wished us to clear out at once.

I endeavoured to make myself friendly to them, and made signs that I was willing to give them knives and tomahawks. But they were at once very timid and very resentful, and no single native would approach near to me, though the whole body of them gradually came closer and closer. I did not feel any fear that they contemplated an attack. My chief dread at the time was, so far as I remember, that some one of my collecting boys should fire a gun and thus frighten away the strangers. I was extremely anxious to get into touch with them and to make friends, partly to get food and partly to enlist their help in my collecting work. On previous expeditions in the hill country of British New Guinea I had obtained the most valuable help from the volunteer native assistants, who had been satisfied to bring me in great numbers of specimens and ample supplies of food in return for some small articles of trade.

As I found that I was not getting on very well with what eloquence I could attempt on natives who understood nothing of what I said, and probably little of my signs, I thought that possibly they would understand my meaning if I showed them some feathers of Birds of Paradise. I went to my tent, therefore, and brought out some plumage and waved it over my head. I then endeavoured, by making noises resembling a gun going off and making signs of a gun being pointed, to show them that I was there to shoot Birds of Paradise. I think the spectacle would have been rather amusing if there had been a white observer. It was successful to this extent, that the natives came somewhat closer. Then I threw towards them a knife and a tomahawk as presents. Promptly they bolted back into the bush. I persevered and gave one of my boys a knife to offer the natives. More cunning than I had been, he threw it, not towards them

IN CENTRAL DUTCH NEW GUINEA 225

directly but across the front of their line, and one of the natives went up to examine the knife. I noticed that he took a handful of moss into his hand before picking it up. Evidently he was afraid of some contamination from its strange magic.

I went back then to my plumes of Birds of Paradise as a means of ingratiating myself with the natives, and, I think, got a little more of their confidence. The children were the most confident, but they were restrained by their elders from following their clear inclination to come right into the camp. Finally some of the male natives came to the clearing, leaving their bows and arrows in the bush, but carrying with them their stone adzes. Physically these natives were very fine specimens, as active as mountain goats, but they did not seem to have very much intelligence, and were extremely timid. I got nothing from them in the way of food as the result of my endearing performance. We were still without fresh vegetables to relieve our dull meals of rice and tinned meat.

There is a stage at which the native is too ignorant or too little curious to be charmed by the white man's gifts, just as there is another stage when he has learned too much to set any particular value upon them. In his absolutely savage and untutored stage the Papuan native has not sufficient education to appreciate the value of what the white man brings. He does not want iron because he has not yet been taught its use. This stage of the native mind is even worse to the white trader, or the white collector, than a later stage, when, from long contact with the white man, the savages have gained as much iron and cloth as they wish for. Once the native has learnt about iron he will covet it until he has enough for his needs. But I have noticed that the native, as soon as he comes to possess iron, promptly degenerates in his old art of carving. The native who has an iron tool never does as good carving as he did before with his rough implements made of shells and animals' teeth.

After this visit of the natives to my camp I waited for a long while, hoping that their curiosity would induce them to come again. But it was in vain. So then I decided that I should return their call. Without telling any of my boys of my intention I went down to the village alone one day. The natives were thrown into a state of violent alarm at my approach. They yelled and screamed, rushed for their weapons, and made signals warning me not to approach. I however, kept on and made signs that I only wanted a smoke. They seemed to understand that as a sign of peace, for they brought tobacco[1] and a pipe, but

---

[1] See footnote on page 115. It may be presumed with some certainty that these hill tribes had never come into contact with white men before, and had, therefore, not got their tobacco plants from Europeans. Nor did they seem to have any communication with the coast tribes. The weight of evidence on this tobacco question—the facts that the hill tribes in New Guinea have native tobacco: and the coast tribes have not until it comes to them from the white man—points to one of two conclusions,

they were still too frightened to allow me to gain their confidence.

Deprived as we were of any food except a small allowance of rice and tinned meat, my whole party was getting very miserable and in a low state of health. Finally, one day I discovered that one of my boys had contracted beri-beri.[1] This disease, which

---

either (1) that the tobacco plant is indigenous to New Guinea, or (2) that the tobacco plant was introduced there from America at a period of which there is no historical record.—EDITOR.

[1] Steady investigations into the causation of beri-beri are being made by the British medical authorities in the South Seas. The Papuan Government medical officer in his 1911 report states—

"Although the staple diet of indentured natives has been rice throughout the Territory, we have been on the whole not much troubled with this disease. Last year about thirty cases occurred at the Lakekamu gold-field, but it disappeared about September, and no further cases were reported till May this year, when the Government medical officer reported eleven cases, with three deaths. The Central District has been apparently free, the cases mentioned in the report on the Native Hospitals having been brought in about August 1910, from Lakekamu. In February, about thirty cases were reported as occurring at Woodlark Island. As I have had no further news from that quarter, I presume that no further cases occurred. In the meantime the Government have been making inquiries from various sources in Eastern Asia, with the result that we gather that the opinion is gaining ground that too highly polished rice is a factor in causing the disease, and that par-boiled or unpolished rice is coming into vogue as an article of diet in place of the more polished article. We also learned that the par-boiled rice on the market is unpalatable, and that the unpolished rice was unattractive in appearance, and a regular supply was uncertain. Assuming that the theory of too highly polished rice was correct, and that a deficiency in phosphatic salts might be a cause of the disease, we considered

shows itself first by a swelling in the lower limbs, a swelling which gradually spreads to the trunk and upwards to the heart, seems to be due to improper feeding; I think it is a species of land scurvy. My boy who contracted the disease complained first of loss of feeling in the legs. Then his legs below the knees began to get puffy and quickly this puffiness spread. When the puffiness gets past the middle of the trunk the patient usually dies. The chief pain seems to be all the while in the stomach. The only remedy so far as I know is a change of diet.

After suffering frightful pain for two days my boy died and I had reason to fear that I would have more cases on my hands. On a previous expedition I had been forced by an outbreak of measles to go away from a fine collecting ground. I was now face to face again with the same notice to quit. I had either to give up the work at a spot which was so promising of good results or make my boys run the risk of death.

---

that the need could be equally well served by adopting the system adopted in the Japanese Navy of adding to the dietary scale foods containing the elements lacking in a rice diet. By substituting a portion of the rice for peas, and adding a small quantity of dripping to the ration scale, we are safeguarding not only in the case of the above-mentioned theory, but two other theories in regard to beri-beri—one that it is due to a deficiency in proteids, and the other that it is due to a deficiency in fats. Last year, when beri-beri was present at Lakekamu, this diet was served out to the police and Crown servants, and no case of beri-beri appeared amongst them. This diet has also been in vogue at the Port Moresby gaol for the past three months, resulting in improved conditions among the prisoners."—EDITOR.

IN CENTRAL DUTCH NEW GUINEA

The decision could only be in the one direction. I decided to start down for the coast.

On the first day down another of my boys showed clear signs of having contracted beri-beri, and next day there was another patient. We camped on the bank of the river at a point ahead of the Canoe Camp, and there the second patient died. Then I made a temporary camp for the third sick boy and sent the other members of the expedition forward to the Canoe Camp with the collections and stores and with instructions to come back and bring us along. As soon as I was alone with the sick boy I found symptoms of illness affecting myself, and I feared that I too had contracted beri-beri. Fortunately that fear proved groundless, but I was very sick indeed, and when the third of my boys died the effect on my spirits was sadly depressing.

I had kept only two of the healthy boys with me, and one of them I sent forward now in the track of the main party and asked him to hurry up the other boys and to bring along a litter in case they had to carry me down to the river. The remaining boy and I then buried the dead and started to walk as best we could towards the Canoe Camp. Through some mistake, I did not meet the boys who were on their way back to help me, and they, coming to the site of the camp that we had abandoned and finding a newly made grave, concluded that I was dead and abandoned the spot in terror. However, we were all reunited at the Canoe Camp, and I soon recovered a fair degree of health. In truth I had been upset by the sight of the death of my boys rather than actually afflicted with any definite disease, though of course I was seriously run down owing to the hardships of the expedition.

I had become very fond of my boys after seeing them working by the side of the Malay coolies of the Dutch : and the Dutch people, too, very greatly admired my boys from British New Guinea for their cheerfulness, endurance and capacity for work. They reckoned they would sooner have fifty of my chaps than a couple of hundred of their own coolies.

After leaving Central Dutch New Guinea in March 1911, I indulged myself in a long spell in Australia, visiting as usual my friends the Barnards. Then I decided to visit London, partly for a conference with the Hon. Walter Rothschild and Dr. Hartert and Dr. Jordan, of the Tring Museum; partly with an idea of following the advice which had been urged on me by friends for many years of preparing for the press a book giving some record of my experiences in the South Sea Islands; but chiefly to pay a visit to my parents.

In undertaking the task of writing a book, I felt that I was entering upon an expedition into absolutely unknown country; not without its dangers probably : not without its hardships certainly. But the urging of friends was insistent : and I came at last to agree with them that there might be some grains of rice to be gathered out of my first-hand impressions of wild life in the South Seas: for I have had opportunities which I think are unique of getting on familiar terms with the natives and with the zoological life in parts of the earth never before explored by a white man. I know that I have not made anything like full use of my opportunities. I can claim neither to be a scientist nor a descriptive writer. But to very many other kindnesses the Hon. Walter Rothschild added that of an offer to contribute an introduction to my book. Then my friends Dr. Hartert and Dr. Jordan, of the Tring Museum, offered to supervise the scientific names and zoological notes in it: and their position in the scientific world made that promise of the greatest value to me. Finally, an old Australian friend agreed to be editor and to pilot me through the writing reefs. So the book was undertaken.

After some months of London—during which a fierce taxi-cab in the Haymarket, missing the taking of my life by the fraction of a second, convinced me that civilisation has also its perils—I am returning to the South Seas, with another ten years, at least, to look forward to of collecting in wild country.

INDEX

ABORIGINALS, Australian, 33–34, 35, 206
Activity of the devil, 188
Adventurous life, desire for, 1
Aegotheles insignis pulcher, 128
Alcohol in tropical climates, 40, 48, 91
Alligator Point, 33
Amido, 39
Angabunga River, 139
Antherea, 98
Antipodes, life in, 38
Aola, 181
Arsenic for skins, 27
Astrapia splendidissima, 221
Attacks by Isurava natives, 167
Australian aboriginals, 33, 34, 35, 206
—— aboriginal, expert water-finder, 206
—— —— weatherwise, 33
—— cattle-man, 10
—— scrubmen, 29
—— summer, 17
—— swan, 164

"Back country," the, 16, 17
Barnard, the Messrs., 5, 6, 8, 10, 21, 22, 27, 39, 73, 74
Barnard Island Rifle Bird, 32
Barnard's Station, 198
Bêche-de-mer, 42
Beri-beri, 217, 227, 228, 229
Biagi, 161
Billabong, 18
Birds hunt moths, 144
—— never hunt butterflies, 144
Birds of Paradise, 32, 37, 49, 99, 122, 132, 149, 150, 162, 163, 213, 225
Black-soil plains, 12
Bladensburg ranges, 18
Bloodshed sometimes necessary, 55
Bloomfield river, 34
"Blossom trees," 105

Bornean canoes, 213
Bougainville, 101, 135, 136, 181, 183, 184
—— kingfisher, 135
Bower-birds, 122, 149, 150
—— birds' playgrounds, 151
Bramble Cay, 201, 202
—— —— sea-birds, 201
Branding cattle, 9
British Ornithologists' Union, 200
Buna Bay, 177
Burgees, 83
Burns, Philp & Co., 210
Bush, the, 11
"Bush lawyer," 159
Bushworker, the, 13
Butterflies and creeks, 124
—— habits of, 151
—— successful lure for, 125
Butterfly breeding, 175
Bwoidunna, 114, 121, 125

Cairns, 168
"Calliope," cutter, 85, 89, 107, 108, 111
Cannibalism, 54, 89, 93, 102, 145, 169
Canoe accident, 212
Cape York, 30, 100
Carpentaria, Gulf of, 23
Carriers, women, 117
Carrion iguana, 29
Cassowary, 138
Cattle camp, 8
—— country, 12
—— friendships, 8
—— life, 7, 14
Cedar Bay, 35, 38, 63
Charagia, 98
—— *eugyna*, 162
—— *marginatus misimanus*, 86
—— *mirablis*, 37, 62
"Charm," cutter, 77
Charm of the jungle, 199
Chibia carbonaria dejecta, 93
Chiefs' head-dresses, 123

233

INDEX

Chinese eaten by cannibals, 89
Choiseul Island natives, 133
Christian Missions, 120
Cinclosoma ajax, 100
"Clean-skins," 21
Climate in Papuan hill districts, 148
Coast people, Papuan, 57
Collecting trips, early, 3, 28, 49
Communication between Papuan villages, 146
Cooktown, 39, 58, 60, 61, 94, 152, 168, 169
―― adventurous voyage, 132
Coomooboolaroo Station, 5, 6, 10, 11, 16, 21, 23, 27
Copra, 191
Couch grass, 101
Crocodile, a carrion feeder, 31
―― eggs of, 28
―― skin, vulnerable, 31
―― venerated, 31
Crocodile's bite, infection of, 322
Crocodiles, 28, 31, 187, 209
Croton hedges, 139
Crowned Pigeon, 100
Cuculus optatus, 125
Currency, coarse salt as, 115, 153, 154
―― pearl shell, 154
―― shell, 73
―― tobacco, 115
Cuscus, 126
Cyclopsittacus virago, 85

Delias, 86
Diamintina River, 18
Disaster from measles, 129
Divers, Japanese, 6
―― white, 6
Dried human hands for ornaments, 57
Droughts, Australia, 12
Droving, 23
Dugong, the, 36
Dutch New Guinea, 179
―― ―― ―― natives, 213
―― ―― ―― climate of, 220
Dysentery, epidemics, 51, 94, 157

Egham Islands, 72
Eichhorns, the, 91, 103, 159
Elderslie, 18
"Ellengowan," schooner, 72
Emancipation of Papuan women, 119

Endoliisoma amboinense tagulanum, 93
Engineer group, 87
Enumakli, chief, 66, 67
E. rostratum, 92
Erythrotriorchis doriae, 176
Eulacestoma nigropectus, 164
Eulepis epignes, 135
Eupetes, species of, 99
"Evil eye," the, 59

Falcinellus striatus, 222
Falco ernesti, 85
Fergusson Island, 44, 45, 81, 85
Ferocity of natives, 168
Fever, 172, 216
Fishing with poison root, 83
―― use of dynamite, 83
"Fleet Wing," 62, 63

Gaol life, 194
Geoffroyas aruensis cyanicarpus, 92
German Mission Station, 185
―― Solomons, 135
Gerygone rosseliana, 92
Giant Rat, 126
Gidyea scrub, 12
Gira River, 59
Giriwa River, 177
Gizo, 133, 182, 190, 193, 195
Goats for meat, 11
Goodenough Island, 77, 81
Goodfellow, Mr., 211
Goodfellow Expedition, 211
"Gooseberry moth," 2
Grandmotherly legislation, 108
Graucalus, 176
―― *hypoleucus louisiadensis*, 93
Grey's observations on Australian aborigines, 35
Grimshaw, Miss Beatrice, 190
Guadalcanar, 102, 104, 136, 181, 191
Gulliver, Mr., 39, 63

Hartert, Dr., 81, 214, 230, 231
Head-hunting, 53
Health notes, 79
"Hekla," 111
―― tragedy, 193, 198
Helcyra chionippe, 161
Hellwig, Mr., 209
Hemiscia meeki, 82
Hibiscus, 106

INDEX

Horse, cunning of, 13
Horses, outlaw, 15
—— and the ways of cattle, 9
Horses' love for cattle work, 10, 22
Hospitality of Papuan mountain tribes, 139
Human life, indifference to, 131
"Humping bluey," 17
Hunting skill of savage races, 204, 205, 207
Hurricanes, 97
Hyde Park, 2

Ilo, 55
Immetalia saturata meeki, 89
Inawa, 112
Inland New Guinea, 137
Inland Solomon Islands collections, 180
Island River, Dutch Expedition, 216, 219

"Jackeroo," 12, 13
Johnson River, 28, 32, 34
Jordan, Dr., 81, 230, 231

Kanakas, 33
—— as collectors, 103
Kangaroo-shooting, 18, 19, 20, 27, 198, 199
Keetava, 77
Keilambete Station, 21, 26
King Edward's death, 203
King snake, 102
Kumusi River, 159

Labour ordinance, 53
Larvae of *Troides chimœra*, 136
Loboparadisea sericea, 222
Loria loriae, 128
Lorius hypoenochrous, 85
Louisiade Group, the, 31

Machaerirhynchus flaviventer novus, 176
Machaerorhamphus alcinus, 176
Macropygia nigrirostris, 82
"Magic," 58, 69, 145, 146, 189
Malaria, 4, 47
M. albigula, 92
Mambaré River, 152, 161
Manna Manna, 111, 122, 133, 137, 139
Manucodia comrii, 85

"Maoheni" (marriage betrothal contract), 118
Marriage by purchase, 117, 120
Marshall, Dr. E., 211
Measles, outbreak of, 127
Meek, Mr. W. G., 74
M. meeki, 143
Melilestes fergussonis, 85
Melirrhophete belfordi griseirostris, 222
Mellopitta lugubris, 128
Melpotes gymnops goliathi, 222
Merauke, 203, 208, 209, 211, 219
Mermaid story, 37
"Merrie Englande," 190
Methodist Mission, 66
Microgoura meeki, 134, 187
Midget wallaby, 126
Milionia elegans, 82
Milne Bay, 96, 97, 98
Mitchell grass, 12
"Mizpah," 60
—— tragedy, 58
Monarcha chalybeocephala, 85
"Moonlighting" cattle, 22
Moosa River tragedy, 80
Morant, Harry, 14
Moths' web as head-dress, 123
Moths, Day-flying, 46, 47
Mound-building birds, 29
Mountains of New Georgia, 181
M. ula, 143
Murderers, law-abiding, 60
Murray, Colonel, 155
"Murua," 89
Myiagra nupta, 93
"Myrtle," barquentine, 39, 61
Myzomela forbesi, 85
Myzomela nigrita louisiadensis, 93

Nabudiga murdered, 166
Nadi, 45, 46, 47, 48, 49, 53, 58, 62, 85, 96
Naphthaline for skins, 27
Nasiterna nanina, 105
Native, carving, 226
—— constabulary, the, 60
—— criers, 148
—— Dubu, 185
—— fear of dogs, 137
—— fishing, 202
—— houses, 45, 46, 96, 102
—— labour, 50, 52, 155, 156, 157
—— love of iron, the, 99

INDEX

Native outrages, 193
—— standard of morality, 120
—— telephone system, 146
—— tobacco pipes, 48
—— vengeance, 94
—— very old, 134
—— wicker work industry, 184
—— women, misunderstandings over, 117
Natives, childlike, 108, 159
—— and value of pearls, 92
—— friendly, 114
—— ingenuity of, 141
—— in hill districts, 145
—— shoot butterflies with bows and arrows, 140
—— sympathetic collectors, 142
—— unfriendly, 223
—— wooing the, 223
Natural History Museum, Kensington, 4
Navigate, learning to, 75
Navigation in South Sea Islands, 44
Nearly battered to death, 84
Nearly lost at sea, 93
"Nerves," 75
Nests, turtle, 204
Nets made with spiders' webs, 140
New Forest, 2, 3, 39, 41
New Georgia, 101
New Guinea, 4, 8, 10, 30, 38, 39, 43, 57, 76, 202
—— cattle-ranching, 100
—— climate of, 39
—— climate on hills, 114
—— method of making fire, 116
—— natives of, 43, 44, 54, 117
—— purse, 43
—— thousands of languages, 122
—— womenfolk, 43, 106, 117, 120
New Hebrides boys, 99
North-west monsoon, 60, 97

Obscene images, 177
Oceania, 4
Oetakwa River, 210, 211, 213, 217
Ogyris meeki, 97, 98
Okuma, 113, 114, 122
Opodiphthera sciron, 120
Ora Bay, 171, 172
Ornithoptera alexandrae, 161
—— blue, 88, 91
—— *chimæra*, 142, 143
—— *meridionalis*, 98

Ornithoptera victoriae, 105
Outcast tribes, 134
Outfitting equipment, 41, 121
"Overlanding," 23, 24
Overstocking, 12
Owen Stanley ranges, 107, 137, 165, 173
Owgarra, 150
Owl, new, 104

Pachycephala alverti, 93
—— *gamblei*, 126
—— *dubia* and *fortis*, 86
Pandanus leaf, 43
Papilio, 98
—— *laglaizei*, 97, 175
—— *mendana acous*, 187
—— *priamus poseidon*, 87, 124
—— *weiskei*, 114
"Papua for the Papuans," 155
Papuans' love of feathers, 122
Paradigalla brevicauda, 221
Paradisea Decora, 78, 81
Parotia carolae meeki, 214
Peak Vale Station, 21
Pearl divers, 92
Pearling industry, 6
Phonygammus hunsteini, 85
"Pidgin" English, 154, 183
Pig-shooting, 27
Pinarolestes, 176
"Pioneer," the cutter, 44
Pitta, the, 34
P. anerythra, 105
Pitta finschi, 81, 85
P. inexpectatus, 105
P. mackloti, 125
Pitta meeki, 91, 92
P. priamus urvillianus, 87
P. rosseliana, 92
Pneumonia, 130, 160
Podargus intermedius, 81, 85
Port Moresby, 111, 127, 149, 171, 194, 201
Pouri-pouri, 70, 71, 103, 144
Prehistoric race, 188
Pseudoptynx solomonensis, 105
Pteridophora alberti, 222
Ptilopus lewisi vicinus, 85
Ptilotis praeripna nigritergum, 222

Recruiting boys, 152, 153
Redcliff Station, 12, 13, 15
Relics of an older people, 176, 177

INDEX

Rendova Island, 134
Rennell Island, 182
—— —— dangers, 196, 197
Rhamphomantis megarhynchus, 176
Rhipidura louisiadensis, 92
—— *setosa nigromentalis*, 93
Rockhampton, 6, 39, 169
Rossel Island, 31, 89, 91, 92, 94, 181
—— —— morals, 90
Rothschild, the Hon. Walter, 5, 27, 37, 38, 61, 74, 101, 134, 173, 197, 221, 230, 231

Sago leaves, roof of, 46
Salvadorina waiginensis, 125
Samarai, 39, 42, 43, 58, 60, 61, 63, 76, 79, 93, 133, 159, 168, 177, 178, 182, 195, 200
San Christoval Island, 192
Sandalwood-getters, 138
Sand iguana, 29
Saturnid, curious, 123
"Saunek," 210
"Scrubbers," 21, 22
Scrub hen, the, 30
Scrub-hen's nest, the, 30
Scrub turkey, the, 39
"Shamrock," the, 171, 177, 190, 210
Sheep country, 12
—— Station, Hughenden, 11
Shooting rapids, 212
Silos, 13
Skulls as adornments, 53
Smith, Mr. Stanniforth, 55, 115, 116
Smoos, Mr., 209
Snaring birds, 149
Snow Mountains, 210, 211, 215
Solomons, canoe houses, 102
Solomon group, Jew's harp, 141
—— Islands, 8, 53, 96, 101, 102, 184
Sorcerer, 58, 69
Sorcerer's impudence, 59
Sorcery, 69, 70, 71, 103
Sores under the feet, 172
South-east monsoon, 97
South Sea Islanders, 6
—— —— Islands, 39
—— —— —— flower life, 106
—— —— —— life, wearied with, 196
Spells, 72
St. Aignan, 86, 88, 89
St. Christabel, 191

St. Joseph River, 139
State control of liquor, 169
Strix tenebricosa, 128
Sudest, 92, 93
Suloya, 73
"Sundowners," 18
"Switchback" country, 113
Sydney, 200
Synoicus plumblus, 176

Taboo marks, 102
Tai-imi, 59, 60
"Talking at" boys, 158
Tanysiptera rosseliana, 91
Tara Cay, 204, 208
Tenaris, 99
Thieves, 57
"Thorn," the, 2
Thursday Island, 171, 203, 204
Tobacco, 48, 226, 227
—— native way of using, 116
—— plant indigenous to New Guinea, 115
"Tomahawk stones," 73
Traders tempted by lonely life to drunkenness, 191
Tragedy at Ilo, 56
Trees, "sugaring," 2
Tring Museum, 1, 38, 81, 134, 168, 170, 180, 182, 196, 199, 210, 214, 217, 230
Trobriand chief, Toulu, 66
—— Island, 61, 62, 63, 65, 72, 76, 77
Trobrianders, 62, 63, 65, 67, 68
Troides alexandrae, 173, 174, 179, 195
—— breeding of, 172
—— *chimœra*, 130, 144, 161, 162
—— *coelestis*, 86
—— *goliath*, 179
—— *larvae*, 173
—— *meridionalis*, 96
—— *rubianus*, 134
Tropical diseases and regular exercise, 4, 40
Tropical Jungle, 42
Troubles with carriers, 112
Turtle, eggs of, 207
Turtles, eating, 207, 208

Urvilliana, 104

"Valk," 210
Van der Van, Captain, 220

INDEX

Van der Vie, Captain, 212
Village hospitality, 149

West Australia, 38
White employee dies, 172
—— squall, 184
—— traders, and marriages with native women, 189
Whitton, Mr., 44
"Wild life," 3

Winton, 18
Woodlark Island, 72, 73, 76, 85
—— —— gold, 73

Yoshiwarra system, 90
Ysabel Island, 104, 193
Yule Island, 137, 201

Zosterops meeki, 93
—— *metcalfei*, 105

Richard Clay & Sons, Limited, London and Bungay.

CPSIA information can be obtained
at www.ICGtesting.com
Printed in the USA
LVHW050931160921
697954LV00003B/149